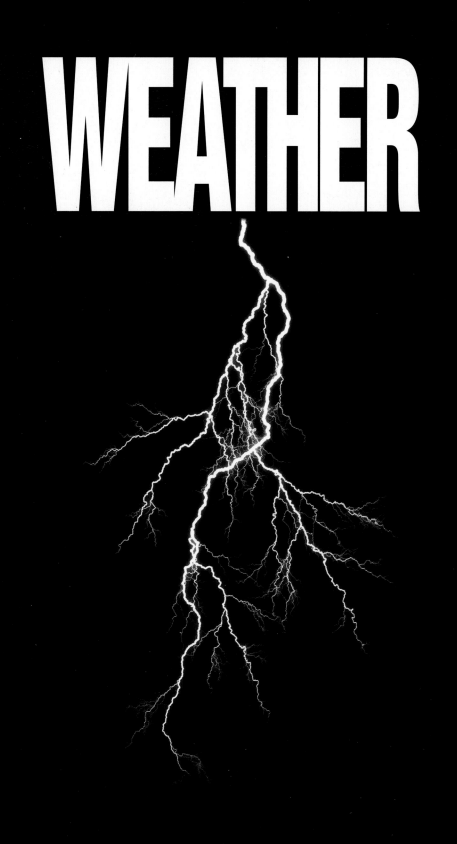

WEATHER

■SCHOLASTIC

Written by John Farndon, Sean Callery,
and Miranda Smith

Designed by Tory Gordon-Harris and Manisha Patel

ISBN 978-1-338-60894-6

10 9 8 7 6 5 4 3 2 1   20 21 22 23 24

Printed in China 62
First edition, October 2020

CONTENTS

FOREWORD

Weather can be wonderful, wild, or just plain weird. It can blast swirling winds, whip up giant waves, freeze the seas, or serve up the dreamiest sunny summer. Yet we are only just beginning to understand this huge force that affects how we feel and behave every day of our lives.

Here on Earth we are just the right distance from the Sun for life to thrive. It is not too hot or too cold, too wet or too dry, too windy or too calm. Earth is sometimes called "the Goldilocks planet" because, like the porridge in the story, it is "just right." Other planets in our solar system are not so lucky—Jupiter's storm, the Great Red Spot, has been battering the planet for at least 350 years, and Venus orbits so close to the Sun that its skies boil.

This book shows how weather works here on Earth, and how our climate (what weather is like on average over a long time) is changing. Humans have built great civilizations, but our activities are altering our planet's atmosphere. All the world's animals and habitats are living through changing times. Never has an understanding of the weather been so vital for our futures.

The first big storm of the year strikes Douro River harbor, Portugal, with wind gusts of 85–95 mph (140–150 km/h), whipping up enormous waves that prevent anyone putting to sea.

EARTH'S WEATHER

All around our planet, held in place by its gravity, is Earth's atmosphere. Weather is what's happening anywhere in the lowest layer, the troposphere (see pp. 16–17). You experience that locally as hot or cold temperatures, water falling as rain or snow, or incredible clouds in the sky. Your experience is one tiny part of a chaotic global system.

SUPER STAR

It is not Earth at all but our star, the Sun, 93,000,000 miles (150 million km) away, that creates most of our weather. Its energy streams through space, its rays striking the Earth at different angles because the planet is round. This creates a restless movement of air and water in the troposphere, in great swirling currents, distributing heat energy across the planet. Much of our world is covered by water. We never lose any and we never gain any. The Sun fuels the process by which ocean water turns into vapor—an invisible watery gas. But, as it cools, the vapor turns back into liquid water to form clouds. Eventually, droplets in the clouds grow bigger and fall as rain, sleet, or snow. And so the cycle begins again. The Sun gives us seasons—as the Earth orbits the Sun, its slight tilt means that different parts of the planet are cooled or warmed, taking us from winter to summer.

Neptune Uranus Saturn Jupiter Mars Earth Venus Mercury

SUN

PERFECT PLANET

Earth orbits the Sun at a distance where the temperature is just right for liquid water to exist. And liquid water is essential for life. Looking for planets in "the Goldilocks zone" is a way that scientists hone their search for other planets with life-forms. Elsewhere in our solar system, however extreme we think our weather is, it's not. Mercury has no atmosphere! Nothing to protect it from the Sun's radiation. Solar winds interact with its magnetic field to form plasma tornadoes. Mars's atmosphere is extremely thin, with temperatures falling to −100°F (−73°C) at night. While over on Saturn, a warm, high stream of gas blows in a six-sided loop at its north pole.

Third of eight
Earth is the third planet from the Sun and its distance from the star is critical. It basks in the Sun's warmth, but is protected by a magnetic field that helps to deflect solar winds and an ozone layer that blocks harmful solar radiation.

Ocean currents
Maybe this turtle will hitch a ride on one of the giant rivers flowing through the oceans, known as ocean currents. Currents have a big impact on our weather. At the oceans's surface, they're driven by the wind. They circulate water in giant loops, on either side of the equator, helping to spread warmth more evenly around the planet. Warm currents can make the weather far to the north or south much milder, while cold currents can bring cool, moist weather to tropical coasts. Deep water currents are driven by changes in saltiness and temperature. These also help spread warmth around the planet but they move at a snail's pace, taking up to a thousand years to move once around planet Earth.

CHANGING WEATHER

Earth's climate has always changed dramatically, veering between times of tropical heat (even at the poles), and an ice age so cold that ice sheets neared the equator! For 10,000 years, though, Earth's climate has been stable and mild. But recent human activities seem to have raised the temperature by 2.07°F (1.15°C). And that's causing chaos.

ANCIENT HISTORY

Ever since it gained an atmosphere, about four billion years ago, Earth has been a "Goldilocks" planet with just enough liquid water and sunshine. But that doesn't mean there haven't been some fairly wild swings in its climate. It seems that, at one point, Earth was truly stuck in the freezer.

Between 600 and 800 million years ago, came an ice age more extreme than anything since. About 55 million years ago, global temperatures spiked as high as 73°F (23°C) on average, and crocodile-like creatures and palm trees lived above the Arctic Circle! At least five ice ages have occurred in Earth's history and we are living in one of them now. For the last 10,000 years, we have been in an "interglacial" period, in which average temperatures have warmed to around 60°F (15°C).

Snowball Earth
Scientists believe that Earth experienced its most severe ice age around 700 million years ago. A massive glaciation engulfed the planet and it remained frozen for at least 120 million years.

TOO FAST

Sometimes, the changes in climate can be so extreme that many species of plants and animals can't cope and die out in mass extinctions. Since 1950, carbon dioxide emissions from human activity have increased by over 400 percent. By far the biggest cause of this is when people burn fossil fuels, such as coal and oil, for energy. Carbon dioxide traps heat in our atmosphere, and Earth is warming up—global temperatures have risen by 2.07°F (1.15°C) in the last 140 or so years. The extra heat is driving record temperatures, reducing snow cover and sea ice, and changing habitats for plants and animals. Heat waves, floods, droughts, wildfires, hurricanes . . . the forecast is for decades of wild weather.

Raging wildfire
As Earth's climate is becoming hotter and drier, wildfires are becoming more frequent and intense. The wildfire season has lengthened across a quarter of the world's burnable surface. Warmer temperatures mean more storms and more lightning, the biggest natural cause of fires.

Destructive power

Extreme weather events have been recorded throughout history, but today, they are becoming more frequent. Here are some of the things we can expect.

Heat waves will become more intense and longer lasting, leading to drought.

Rainfall will become more variable and more extreme, with flooding more common.

Big, destructive hurricanes are striking the US three times more frequently than they did 100 years ago.

EXTREME WEATHER

It may surprise you, but by far the most weather-related deaths and injuries in the United States every year are caused by extreme heat in heat waves. On these pages are some of the most recent dangerous weather events around the world.

Blizzards

In February 2010 in North America, two blizzards broke snowfall records—32.4 ins (82.3 cm) at Washington's Dulles Airport and, after the storms, 68.1% of the country was blanketed with snow.

Hailstorm

A hailstorm with baseball-sized hailstones struck at rush hour in Denver, Colorado, on May 8, 2017, trapping people in cars and buses—the most destructive Colorado storm, with more than $2.3 billion in damages.

Hailstones can be up to 8 ins (20 cm) in diameter.

Wildfires

The town of Paradise was devastated in less than a day by a particularly fierce wildfire, part of the Camp Fire in northern California, that lasted from November 8 to 25, 2018. At least 85 people died, 153,336 acres (62,053 hectares) burned, 18,804 buildings were destroyed, and there was $7.5–10 billion in damages.

Hurricane

The Category 4 Hurricane Maria made landfall on September 20, 2017, near Yabucoa, Puerto Rico. Afterward, the whole of Puerto Rico was declared a Federal disaster zone, with 2,975 dead and $90 billion in damages.

Drought

In November 2019, several regions of southern Africa were declared drought disaster areas as some had gone without substantial rainfall for up to five years. Experts say this was the worst drought in 1,000 years.

CHANGING HISTORY

Weather has played a part in some major landmarks in human history. In 1588, in one of the most decisive battles of all time, Philip II of Spain set sail against Elizabeth I of England. The crescent shape of his fleet was blown to pieces by a fierce wind driving his ships northward. In 1776, fog over New York's East River hid the army led by General George Washington as they escaped the British army who might otherwise have stopped the American Revolution in its tracks. Weather contributed to the sinking of the *Titanic* in April 1912, increasing iceberg hazards on that fateful day. Perhaps the most important weather forecast ever was made in June 1944. The Allies were preparing to invade western Europe and defeat the Nazi forces. In early June, Group Captain James Stagg and his team from Britain's Met Office identified bad weather, which resulted in the postponement of invasion on June 5, and identified a window of better weather allowing it to go ahead on June 6. When asked why the Normandy invasion had succeeded, US President Eisenhower said: "Because we had better meteorologists than the Germans."

Floods
Unusually high monsoon rainfall caused the worst floods in nearly a century in July and August 2018 in the south Indian state of Kerala. At least 430 people died, and there were billions of dollars' worth of damage.

Bushfires
The worst wildfires in decades during the bushfire season of 2019–2020 affected large areas of Australia, but particularly New South Wales. At least 31.1 million acres (12.6 million hectares) burned, more than 33 people died, and many thousands of homes were destroyed.

Typhoon
One of the most powerful tropical cyclones ever recorded hit Palau, Micronesia, the Philippines, Vietnam, and South China in November 2013. Typhoon Haiyan killed more than 6,300 and cost more than $5.8 billion in damages.

RESTLESS

AIR

EARTH'S ATMOSPHERE

OUR PLANET'S LIFE JACKET

Without the atmosphere, Earth's blanket of gases, this would be a dead planet. The atmosphere not only gives us air to breathe. It also stops Earth freezing by holding on to the Sun's heat. And it shields living things from the Sun's deadlier rays. There are five or so layers to the atmosphere, but it's the troposphere, the lowest layer, in which all our weather happens.

Highest layer
Earth's atmosphere thins out with each higher layer until it reaches space and dissipates at an altitude known as the Kármán line, about 62 miles (100 km) above the surface. Not all scientists agree that the exosphere, the highest layer, is really part of Earth's atmosphere—they consider it part of the space into which the atmosphere eventually fades.

What's in the atmosphere?
Earth's atmosphere is a colorless mixture of gases, water, and dust. It is mainly nitrogen and oxygen, with small amounts of argon, carbon dioxide, and other trace gases. The water content varies with temperature; most of the atmosphere's water is in the troposphere.

Oxygen 21%

Argon 0.93%

Nitrogen 78%

Trace gases 0.04%

Trace gases

Neon 4.7%

Helium 1.3%

Methane 0.4%

Nitrous oxide 0.08%

Carbon dioxide 93.5%

ATMOSPHERIC GASES BY VOLUME

INCREASING ALTITUDE

DECREASING ALTITUDE

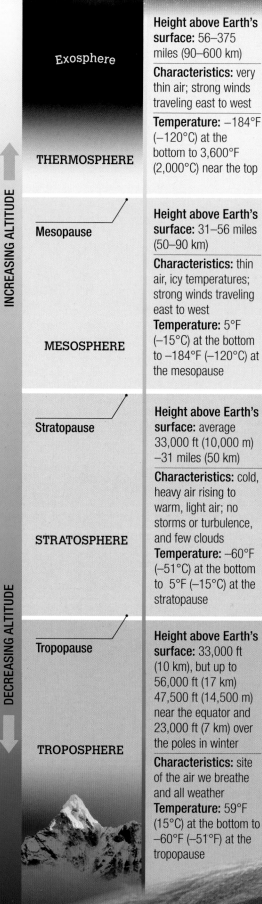

Exosphere

THERMOSPHERE

Height above Earth's surface: 56–375 miles (90–600 km)

Characteristics: very thin air; strong winds traveling east to west

Temperature: −184°F (−120°C) at the bottom to 3,600°F (2,000°C) near the top

Auroras
The flickering colored lights known as auroras (see pp.18–19) are normally seen in the thermosphere.

Mesopause

MESOSPHERE

Height above Earth's surface: 31–56 miles (50–90 km)

Characteristics: thin air, icy temperatures; strong winds traveling east to west

Temperature: 5°F (−15°C) at the bottom to −184°F (−120°C) at the mesopause

Meteorite trails
Shooting stars are the fiery trails of meteorites burning up in the mesosphere.

Stratopause

STRATOSPHERE

Height above Earth's surface: average 33,000 ft (10,000 m) –31 miles (50 km)

Characteristics: cold, heavy air rising to warm, light air; no storms or turbulence, and few clouds

Temperature: −60°F (−51°C) at the bottom to 5°F (−15°C) at the stratopause

Polar clouds
There are few clouds because the stratosphere is very dry, but polar stratospheric clouds (PSCs, above) form near the poles in winter.

Tropopause

TROPOSPHERE

Height above Earth's surface: 33,000 ft (10 km), but up to 56,000 ft (17 km) 47,500 ft (14,500 m) near the equator and 23,000 ft (7 km) over the poles in winter

Characteristics: site of the air we breathe and all weather

Temperature: 59°F (15°C) at the bottom to −60°F (−51°F) at the tropopause

High fliers
Airliners mostly cruise at 35,000 ft (10,670 m), where the air is calmer and offers less resistance, saving fuel.

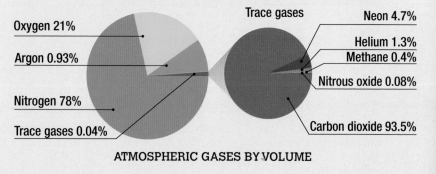

THERMOSPHERE

THINNEST AND HOTTEST

Though gases in the thermosphere are incredibly thin, they absorb ultraviolet (UV) rays from the Sun, creating high temperatures. This layer is also called the ionosphere because it contains electrically charged particles (ions).

ISS

In orbit

On average, the International Space Station (ISS) orbits 250 miles (400 km) above Earth's surface. The atmosphere here is very thin, but there is still enough air to cause drag: Each month, the ISS has to adjust for about 1.2 miles (2 km) lost in altitude due to drag.

MESOSPHERE

COLDEST LAYER

Mesosphere gases are too thin to absorb much heat energy from the Sun, so temperatures fall rapidly with altitude, making this the coldest layer. But there is still enough gas here to slow down meteorites and cause sufficient friction to make them burn up.

Sounding rocket

Research by rocket

The mesosphere is difficult to study because weather balloons and aircraft cannot fly high enough, so scientists launch "sounding rockets" to collect data. For example, the rockets can release a compound that creates white, expanding clouds. From the clouds' shape, scientists can calculate the level of turbulence in the mesosphere.

STRATOSPHERE

THE CALM LAYER

With no turbulence or storms to mix things up here, warm, light air rises above cold, heavy air. It gets hotter the higher you go, and the air at the top is 1,000 times thinner than at sea level. The stratosphere holds the ozone layer, Earth's filter for harmful UV radiation.

Balloon investigators

Weather balloons are tied to sondes, instrument boxes that collect data every 6 ft (2 m) as they float into the stratosphere. The balloons expand as they rise and eventually burst.

Blue jet

A rare type of of lightning occurs in the stratosphere. Called a "blue jet," it emerges from the tops of thunderstorms and can travel from the bottom to the top of the stratosphere at 22,370 mph (36,000 km/h). Exactly what causes this bright blue streak is a mystery.

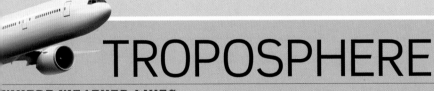

TROPOSPHERE

WHERE WEATHER LIVES

About 80 percent of the atmosphere's mass—including gases, water, and dust—is in the troposphere, all stirred up by heat to create weather. "Tropos" means change: Air in this layer cools by 3.5°F per 1,000 ft (6°C per 1,000 m) of altitude.

Clouds

Different types of clouds form at different levels (see pp.56–57). Thin, wispy cirrus clouds form high up, layered stratus and puffy cumulus clouds appear low down. Anvil clouds are towering cumulonimbus clouds that stretch right up to the tropopause.

Anvil cloud

Northern lights

Winter nights are long and dark in northern Canada, Alaska, Siberia, Greenland, and Scandinavia. But occasionally, pitch-black polar skies here are lit up by nature's most spectacular light show—the aurora, pictured here in Iceland. Light shows like these hang in the skies above both ends of the Earth. In the north they're known as the aurora borealis, or northern lights, and in the south as the aurora australis, or southern lights.

Auroras flash into view when electrically charged particles streaming from the Sun collide at incredible speeds with particles of gas in Earth's atmosphere. They occur above the poles because this is where there is a deep cleft in Earth's magnetic field or magnetosphere. Elsewhere, the magnetosphere protects the planet from solar bombardment, but around the poles the shield is weak and the solar assault streaks in. The polar cleft is roughly oval, and so from space, the auroras form huge, crownlike rings. Auroras appear in various forms, from a broad glow beyond the horizon to streamers, arcs, and rippling curtains, lighting up the night in vivid colors. The stream of solar particles is called the solar wind and it erupts from sunspots on the Sun's surface. Sunspots seem to reach a peak every 11 years, and the most spectacular auroras coincide with these sunspot peaks.

WATER IN THE AIR

CONTINUAL MOTION

The atmosphere is the world's biggest sponge. You cannot see it, but there are 37.5 million billion gallons of water floating invisibly in the air as vapor. And that is not including the water you can see in the countless droplets that make clouds. Water vapor is found only in the troposphere, the atmosphere's lowest layer, and it is here that all weather happens.

Earth's water supply in total: 332.5 million cubic miles (1.386 billion cubic km)

Saltwater as percentage of Earth's surface water: 96.5%

Water frozen as ice: 2%

Water trapped underground: 0.5%

Freshwater: only a small fraction of Earth's water is freshwater

Life-giving water
Water is older than Earth itself, and some may be older than the Sun. It came here long ago and no one knows how. All the water in the world today is that same ancient water, used over and over again.

Getting vaporized
The Sun has to beam in 17,000 calories of energy to vaporize one ounce (28 g) of water. This is what kickstarts the world's weather. When this vapor condenses back into water again, it releases its energy back into the atmosphere. There is enough energy locked up in the atmosphere's water to power a big city for hundreds of millions of years.

Dew collecting around the edge of a leaf

Close-up of dew on blade of grass

Dew point
How does air take up so much water? The answer is that it fits into spaces between the molecules. When there is no space left, the air is saturated and can take no more—unless it gets warmer, and the spaces enlarge. When air gets colder, however, the spaces shrink, and the vapor is squeezed out and forced to condense into liquid water. The point at which this happens is called the dew point.

Water-go-round

Water makes weather happen because it is constantly changing state. Saltwater in the oceans is ancient. However, freshwater hangs in the air, falls as rain, runs into rivers and lakes, and then runs back to the sea, changing from solid ice to liquid water to gaseous vapor and back again all the time. This big loop is called the water cycle. Weather is the water cycle in action.

Cloud formation
Water vapor is carried up by rising warm air, then cools and condenses to make clouds.

Makeup of clouds
Clouds are drops of water and crystals of ice that are so light they float.

Sun's heat
The Sun warms the oceans, evaporating some of the water into vapor.

Rising vapor
Water also evaporates, or transpires, from the leaves of plants.

Precipitation
When cloud drops grow too big, they fall as rain and snow.

Runoff
Most rain runs off into rivers and streams and back to the oceans.

Watering plants
Some rain soaks into the ground where plants suck it up through their roots.

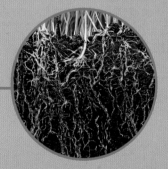

Wet, wet, wet

The proportion of water vapor in the air, its humidity, is constantly changing. Clear blue skies are generally dry with low humidity, most obviously above deserts, but often also in spring, or when the wind blows from the east. Rising humidity thickens the sky, making it mistier. Tropical rain forests are often wreathed in

Water vapor rising from the Costa

Clear blue sky above desert sands

Relatively moist

If air is warm, it can still look vivid blue and clear even when its humidity is high. That is because the moisture it can hold varies with temperature. So weather experts talk about "absolute humidity"—the total amount of moisture in the air. And there is also "relative humidity," which is how much moisture there is compared to the total it could hold at the temperature. This

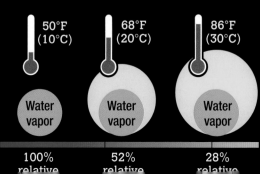

50°F (10°C)	68°F (20°C)	86°F (30°C)
Water vapor	Water vapor	Water vapor
100% relative	52% relative	28% relative

SPREADING SUNSHINE

LIFE-GIVING ENERGY

Every hour, the Sun bombards the Earth with 430 quintillion joules of energy! That's more than the entire human world uses in a year. It passes through the atmosphere mostly as light and infrared (heat) rays, producing the stunning brilliance of daylight as it scatters off the air. But when it hits Earth's surface, it warms the land and the oceans, stirring up the planet's great stew of weather.

Spreading sunshine

The atmosphere may look delicate, but it actually stops almost half the Sun's rays. Only 52 percent make it through all the way to the ground, while 23 percent is absorbed (soaked up) by the atmosphere in clouds, water vapor, gases, and dust. The rest is reflected (bounces back) into space. This split of the Sun's energy is called Earth's "solar energy budget."

17 percent
of solar radiation is reflected back into space by clouds.

The Sun's rays

The Sun is a giant nuclear reactor blasting out a ferocious array of radiation toward Earth nonstop, and 41 percent of this radiation is visible light. Half comes in waves too long to see, such as infrared. Fortunately, the upper atmosphere shields us from most of the remaining 9 percent—dangerous shortwave radiation such X-rays, gamma rays, and ultraviolet rays.

Greenhouse effect
Like a greenhouse, gases in Earth's atmosphere hold in the warmth needed for life to flourish.

Greenhouse Earth

Despite the Sun's power, Earth would be icy cold were it not for a few special gases in the atmosphere, including carbon dioxide (CO_2), water vapor, and methane. These gases absorb and re-radiate infrared heat waves, trapping warmth radiating from the ground that would otherwise be lost to space. This is called the "greenhouse effect" because, like glass in a greenhouse, the gases let sunlight in but stop its warmth from escaping again. Scientists call the sun power that hits the ground insolation.

Ground effect

Some of the Sun's energy is reflected coolly away from the Earth's surface. But some is soaked up, then slowly released as heat. It's this heat that drives weather. But while some surfaces soak up a lot of Sun energy and release it as heat, others reflect most of it away. This chart shows the percentage reflected away by different surfaces. This measurement is called "albedo."

5%

8%

20%

Sunlight takes about 8.3 minutes to reach Earth from the Sun.

100%

23 percent
is absorbed by our atmosphere— 4 percent clouds and 19 percent water vapor, gases, and dust.

8 percent
is reflected back into space by atmospheric gases and dust.

6 percent
is reflected by Earth's surface.

52%

46 percent
is directly absorbed by Earth's surface (land and water). Ocean water is evaporated in the water cycle.

Hot stuff
When the Earth's surface slowly releases the heat it has absorbed from sunshine, it warms the air above. This gives the air the energy to drive weather and creates every weather effect, from gale-force winds to pelting rain. Heat makes air molecules move faster. The hotter it is, the faster and more energetically they move. Temperature is the measure of just how fast air molecules are moving.

Average temperatures
The way that sunlight hits Earth's surface is illustrated by this map of average annual temperatures. The Sun's rays strike most directly at the equator, so those areas are the hottest (red). The cold areas of the poles are shown in blue and purple.

HOTTEST AND COLDEST PLACES

134.06°F (56.7°C)
Death Valley, California

−128.6°F (−89.2°C)
Vostok research station, Antarctica

30%

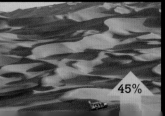

45%

90%

The poles
Polar regions have the highest albedo because their bright snow and ice reflect the most sunlight

Taking the temperature

Air temperature has to be measured in the shade, as direct sunlight can give a falsely high reading. Meteorologists put the thermometer inside a Stevenson screen, a box with ventilation slots. Temperature is measured in Fahrenheit, Celsius, or Kelvin. A temperature of 0 Kelvin (equal to −459.67°F or −273.15°C) is called absolute zero, and it's the lowest temperature anything can reach!

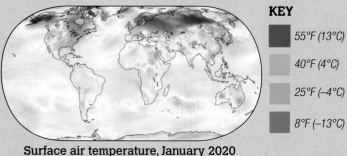

KEY

■	55°F (13°C)
■	40°F (4°C)
■	25°F (−4°C)
■	8°F (−13°C)

Surface air temperature, January 2020

Average temperatures

To get a daily average for temperatures, meteorologists add readings for every hour of the day, then divide by 24. For a monthly average, they add the daily averages and divide by the number of days. That is how they knew January 2020 was the hottest January ever recorded.

TEMPERATURE
BIG DIFFERENCES

Are you wearing a sweater today? Air temperature affects how we live! It's generally measured at 4 ft (1.2 m) above the ground. It varies wildly depending on where you're living, whether you're in a city, how near you are to the ocean, and how high you are. It's the variation in temperature that turns the atmosphere into an engine for weather.

Cold, cold, cold

January 2020 was Alaska's coldest January since 2012 and tied with 1970 as the 13th coldest on record. Residents shivered in −6.2°F (−21°C). But much of the rest of the world was having the warmest January since record-keeping began.

Cool heights

Mountaintops are always cold, and some are permanently covered in snow. But it's not just mountain peaks that are chilly. All air usually gets colder the higher you go and the farther away it is from the warm ground. The heat loss with height is steady, typically 1°F (0.6°C) for every 330 ft (100 m).

Hot, hot, hot

The temperature hits a high in Sydney, Australia, every year during February, with an average of 72.1°F (22.3°C). However, partly because of runaway bushfires, on January 4, 2020, the Sydney suburb of Penrith became the hottest place on Earth, with a high of 120.02°F (48.9°C).

Heat movement

Heat is never still. Wherever one place is hotter than another, you can be sure that heat will flow to the cooler place. This is what drives the movement of air around the atmosphere. It happens in three ways: conduction, convection, and advection.

Shiver and shake

Heat is the energy of moving molecules. Conduction is molecules passing on movement to neighbors with a direct, knock-on effect. When the ground is warmed by the Sun during the day, it conducts heat to the thin layer of air above, sometimes making it really hot. At night, the air loses heat back to the cold ground by conduction, and a mist can form.

Up and away

Earth's surface heats the air by conduction, but as the air warms, it expands and becomes lighter (less dense). Soon, it lifts off like a hot-air balloon and floats up into the cooler, denser air above. This is called convection, and it is these rising blobs of air that often create clouds. In the same way, cold air can sink. So the air is going up here and down there, circulating vertically all the time.

Side to side

Air does not only move up and down—it can move sideways, too, taking its properties with it. When a mass of warm air moves sideways, it takes its warmth with it. This is called advection, and it happens on a huge scale. Advection fog forms when warm and moist air is moved over a colder surface, such as a cool sea current, which chills the air to dewpoint, and creates fog (see pp. 74–75).

Day and night

Every 24 hours, Earth spins 360°— everywhere on Earth turns to face the Sun, then turns away again, giving us the everyday miracle of day and night. Earth spins from west to east. So, every day, the Sun comes up in the east and goes down in the west. The effect is that at any one time, half the Earth is bathed in sunlight, while the other is plunged into darkness.

This constant alternation between night and day, dark and light, heating and cooling has a huge effect on the weather. Indeed, all life on Earth responds to this diurnal (daily) rhythm. The most obvious diurnal change is in temperature. Plotted on a graph, daily temperature follows an S-shape, gradually rising toward noon, then sinking through the night. The daily warming always lags behind the Sun, though. The highest temperatures come midafternoon, because the ground has first to warm up, then the ground must warm the air. Similarly, the night is coldest just before dawn, because the ground lets go of its warmth gradually.

In some places, the diurnal variation is dramatic. In some deserts, days are baking hot, while heat is lost quickly into the clear air after sunset, meaning a daily temperature range of 104°F (40°C) or more.

SUN IN THE SKY

THE LIFE-GIVER

If you think the Sun comes up every day, you are wrong. The Sun actually stays perfectly still. It's Earth doing all the moving, spinning like a top every day and hurtling right around the Sun in a vast loop every year. As we move, we get an ever-changing view of our star. So the Sun seems to moves through the sky, controlling our weather like turning a heater up and down.

Day arc

Every day, the Sun appears to take a curving path through the sky, which scientists call the "day arc." After the Sun rises, it arcs higher and higher through the morning, and swings around to the south in the northern hemisphere, or to the north in the southern hemisphere. The Sun reaches its highest point at midday, then slides lower and farther west until sunset.

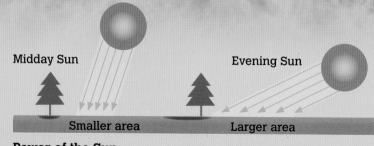

Midday Sun

Evening Sun

Smaller area

Larger area

Power of the Sun

The Sun's power varies throughout the day because of the changing angle at which it hits the ground. It is strongest and most concentrated when high in the sky and shining directly on the ground. It is much weaker when it is lower because its rays are spread out. So it is weakest in the early morning, strong at midday, then gets weaker as it sinks toward sunset.

WHAT COLOR IS THE SKY?

Blue sky thinking

The Sun is a ball of fire. So why is the sky blue? The answer is that light from the Sun contains all the colors of the rainbow. When it hits the gases and particles in Earth's atmosphere, it is scattered in all directions. But blue light has much shorter waves than the other colors, so it gets scattered much, much more, and it is this scattered blue that we see.

Red sky at night

The sky is blue in the day, but often turns red or orange at sunset and sunrise. That is because as the Sun gets lower in the sky, its light has to travel through a lot more of the particles in the atmosphere to reach your eyes. By the time it does, blue and the other shorter waves have been entirely scattered away, leaving only reds and yellows visible to you.

Sunny days in the tropics

Tropical heat, polar chill

The day arc varies depending on how far you are from the equator. The arc is highest and steepest in the tropics, and lowest and shallowest at the poles. So the tropical sun is strong and the weather there is mostly warm; the polar sun is very weak and the weather there is mostly cold. In between is the temperate zone, which can be warm in summer and cool in winter.

Frozen landscape in the Arctic

SEASONS

LEANING TOWARD THE SUN

You can blame all the seasons, from scorching summer to chilly winter, on Earth's yearlong voyage around the Sun! Each season begins when Earth reaches a particular point on its journey. Earth tilts—always in the same direction—so when it's on one side of the Sun, it tilts in, and when it's on the other side, it tilts out. This makes the world's hot spots shift from north to south and back again, and the seasons move with them.

The four seasons

Because Earth is tilted, the angle sunlight strikes it changes continuously as it goes around the Sun. So the angle you see the Sun in the sky from where you live varies, too. The effect is that the Sun's power and the length of the day change throughout the year. When the Sun is high and hot, and days are long, we get summer. When it is low and cool, and days are short, we get winter. Spring and autumn come in between.

March
The Earth's hotspot moves back north again. It reaches the equator around March 21. Days and nights even out. Winter warms into spring in the north, and the weather is changeable and often showery. In the south, autumn begins.

Northern spring, southern autumn

June
As the northern hemisphere tilts toward the Sun, it is summer here, with longer days. Days are often hot and nights warm, and rain falls in afternoon thunderstorms or not at all. But it is winter in the southern hemisphere.

Northern summer, southern winter

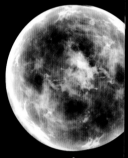

In full leaf during summer

Extreme winters

Many of the bitterest winters are linked to the polar jet stream—a superfast river of air that runs around the Arctic, high in the atmosphere. When kinks in the stream meander south, they drag along icy polar air, bringing Arctic conditions to places like Chicago. Ironically, warm temperatures in the Arctic make the jet stream swing wildly, so global warming may make winters in northeast America extra severe, with terrifying bomb cyclones (see pp. 102–103) that bring blizzards.

Earth's tilt causes seasons—not whether it is **nearer** the **Sun** or **farther away** from it.

Ready to bud in spring

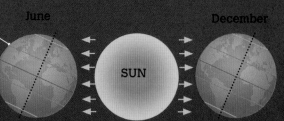
Tropic of Cancer
Equator
Tropic of Capricorn
June
December
SUN

Moving tropics
Earth faces the Sun most directly in the tropics. That's why they're usually very warm. The place on Earth where the Sun is overhead moves farther north between December and June, and farther south from June to December. Its northerly limit is a line called the Tropic of Cancer, and its southerly limit is the Tropic of Capricorn. The tropical zone lies between these limits, and the equator runs through its middle.

Bare and dormant during winter

December
The farther south beyond the equator the overhead Sun moves, the hotter the south becomes, bringing summer. But as the Sun climbs in southern skies, it drops even lower in the sky in the north. Northern nights get longer and winter's icy chill sets in.

Northern winter, southern summer

Equinoxes
Two days in the year, —March 21 and September 23—have days and nights of equal length. These are called equinoxes.

September
The northern hemisphere is tilting away from the Sun. The weather is cooler here, and damp, chilly nights bring morning mists. The weather is often stormy. Meanwhile, spring comes to the south.

Northern autumn, southern spring

Solstices and equinoxes
The Sun's path through the sky shifts with the seasons. Its highest path comes at the summer solstice, which brings the longest day; its lowest path is at the winter solstice, the shortest day of the year. When the Sun crosses the equator, in March and September, there is an equinox, when day and night are equally long—12 hours each—throughout the world.

Dry season
Wet season

Leaves about to fall in autumn

Wet and dry
Only temperate regions have four seasons. Most tropical regions have either no marked season at all, or just a wet season when most of the rain falls, and a dry season. The tropics always get plenty of the Sun's light and heat.

AIR MASSES

Sometimes, weather is completely dominated by giant blobs of air. These monster blobs are called "air masses" and they can be thousands of miles across. They form when light winds let the air sit still long enough to match its environment, and become equally warm or cold, and equally moist or dry throughout.

Mass movement

While wind stays light, air masses bring stable weather. But as soon as the wind picks up a little, an air mass and weather can be blown to a new place. Sometimes it can be driven slap-bang into another air mass with very different temperature and moisture levels. Collisions between air masses like this are one of the main causes of storms.

Mass movement

Weather satellites scan the whole Earth regularly, providing information that warns of severe weather and saves thousands of lives. This frame is from a loop of images taken by a geostationary weather satellite and shows air masses moving from the Atlantic across northern Europe.

Arctic maritime (mA)

When air sits for a while over the bleak, icy waste of the Arctic ice cap, it gets very cold and dry. The Arctic may be an ocean, but it is mainly frozen. When Arctic maritime air slides into northern Canada or Siberia, it brings with it intense cold, and when it oozes south over warmer seas, watch out for snow!

Polar maritime (mP)

Polar maritime air masses are cool and damp. In the northern hemisphere, they start over Greenland; in the southern hemisphere, above the Southern Ocean. They start off chilly, but get warmer and damper as they move over the ocean, bringing damp days in the midlatitudes.

Polar continental (cP)

These winter air masses emerge from the chilly heartlands of Siberia and Canada. It gets seriously raw in winter here, far inland from the softening of the oceans. As the air masses spread out, they bring cold and dry weather with clear, frosty days. Sometimes, they cross water, and then they bring snow.

Source power

Air masses get their name tags from where they come from—their source regions: Equatorial, tropical, polar, and arctic. Equatorial air masses, naturally, develop near the equator, and are warm. Tropical air masses come from the tropics, and are fairly warm, too. Cool polar air masses start in the high-latitudes, while icy Arctic air masses form in the Arctic. Moist air masses form over oceans and are also known as maritime air masses. Dry air masses that develop over land are continental air masses.

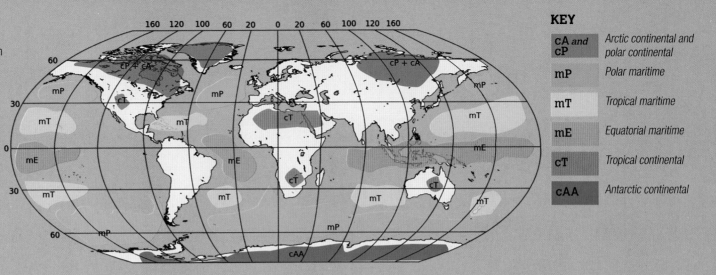

KEY

cA and **cP**	Arctic continental and polar continental
mP	Polar maritime
mT	Tropical maritime
mE	Equatorial maritime
cT	Tropical continental
cAA	Antarctic continental

Antarctic continental (cAA)
This amazingly dry, bitterly cold air only occurs over the continent of Antarctica. When it spreads out across the sea in the Southern Ocean, it takes up water and becomes a cool, moist polar maritime air mass. This brings a damp chill to southern South America, Africa, and Australasia.

Equatorial maritime (mE)
Equatorial air masses are hot and sticky. They originate 15 degrees (latitude) either side of the Equator. They are what brings thunderstorms to tropical rain forests. Air from equatorial air masses meets at low levels to form a band of powerfully rising air known as the Intertropical Convergence Zone.

Tropical continental (cT)
This desert air gets cooked over hot, dry land and spreads out, bringing superhot weather. When there is a drought, the chances are that a tropical continental air mass is to blame. In summer, masses like this may spread from the Sahara Desert into Europe bringing heat waves and dusty, sometimes orange skies.

Tropical maritime (mT)
These warm, moist air masses develop over subtropical oceans and flow toward Europe and the Americas. As they slide over cool oceans, they take up more moisture. They bring mild weather with low clouds and drizzle, and sometimes even fog to coastal regions.

WEATHER FRONTS

WAR ABOVE YOUR HEAD

Weather is basically a huge, global war between competing air masses. They jostle to and fro, growing and shrinking, flowing this way and that. A change in the weather indicates that a different air mass has come your way. The places they meet are the battle lines of the atmosphere, called fronts, and the conflict generates huge storms.

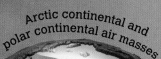

Arctic continental and polar continental air masses

Polar maritime air mass

Polar maritime air mass

Tropical continental air mass

Tropical maritime air mass

Tropical maritime air mass

Tropical maritime air mass

War of the air

Air masses and fronts were discovered by Norwegian meteorologist Jacob Bjerknes in 1919; before then, people thought that weather only changed locally. But Bjerknes realized that weather was actually created by great masses of air sweeping around the world, creating storms where they meet. Bjerknes called these turbulent boundary zones "fronts" after the lines where opposing armies fought in World War I.

Squalls can travel quickly, at speeds up to 60 mph (96.5 km/h)

A squall line crosses the United States

Incoming storm

Squall lines are dramatic lines of storms that develop along a cold front or a dry front. Here, the gust front of a squall is moving across the Pacific Ocean, off the coast of Nicaragua.

Severe squalls

Squalls can look terrifying as they roll over in gigantic walls of clouds. They can stretch for hundreds or even thousands of miles and last for many hours. They can throw everything at you including rain, hail, lightning, and possibly tornadoes and waterspouts.

Cold front

Cold fronts are the atmosphere's bulldozers. They occur where a cold mass is shoving its way forward against warm, moist air and replacing it with cooler, drier air. They move fast, typically at 20–25 mph (32–40 km/h), usually going eastward. As it pushes forward, the cold air drives a wedge under the warm air, lifting it sharply into the air. The warm, moist air shoots up to pile up towering thunderclouds, unleashing short downpours and fearsome gusts of wind.

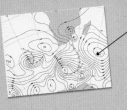

Cold fronts are marked on weather maps with a spiked blue line. The spikes point in the direction of movement.

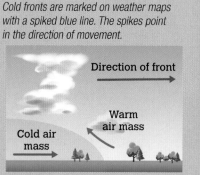

Thunderstorm with lightning along a cold front

Warm front

Warm fronts are the stealth army. Here, warmer, moist air catches up with cold air and slides up gently over it—a process called overrunning—and gradually eases it out of the way. They too give rain, but it is gentler and more prolonged. Warm fronts generally form on the east of storms. With no power to push, they move slowly—at 10–15 mph (16–24 km/h)—so slowly that they are frequently caught up by pursuing cold fronts.

Warm fronts are marked on weather maps with a red line of rounded humps. The humps point in the direction of movement.

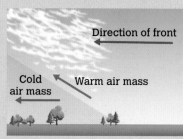

Slow-moving clouds along a warm front

Stationary front

Warm fronts sometimes run up against cold fronts moving the opposite way and both come to a dead stop. In this standoff, the skies fill with clouds, and it starts to rain, and goes on raining! Finally, kinks begin to emerge in the front, and a wave of low pressure ripples along the front and it all starts to move again.

Stationary fronts are marked on weather maps with a line of alternating blue spikes and red humps.

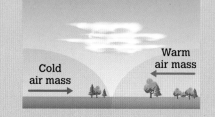

The cloudy sky of a stationary front threatening rain

Occluded front

Occluded basically means blocked or shut up. That's just what an occluded front is—a blockage. It forms when a runaway cold front finally catches up with a slower-moving warm front. The cold front can't undercut the cold air beneath the warm front, so instead it rides up over the top. Everything gets mixed up and for a while rain comes teeming down.

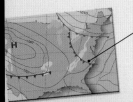

Occluded fronts are marked on weather maps with a purple line of alternating spikes and humps.

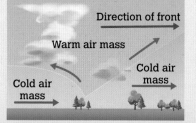

A rainburst from the blockage of an occluded front

Air wars

North America gets especially dramatic and varied weather because it sits right in the battle zone between warm air from the south and cold air from the north.

In summer, warm air pushes northward from the Atlantic Ocean, the Gulf of Mexico, and the Pacific Ocean. It brings mild and pleasant weather to much of the eastern USA. Dry air from Central America wedges its way up to keep things hot and thirsty.

In winter, the tables are turned. Icy air from the snowy wastes of northern Canada pushes its way southward bringing a chill over the Midwest. But because it's hemmed in by the Rocky Mountains in the west and the Appalachian Mountains in the east, it keeps the northern coastal areas milder. Polar air sweeps in continually off the oceans, bringing frequent rain and snow.

This picture of downtown Chicago shows the battle in full flow, as cold polar air jostles with warm, moist air from the south. The cold air undercuts the warmer air, forcing it upward. As the warm air hurls upward, its moisture cools and condenses into dark, billowing rolls of ominous clouds. This is called a cold front and will soon unleash a torrent of rain, gusts of wind, and maybe a few flashes and cracks of lightning and thunder, too.

HIGHS AND LOWS

THE WIND MACHINE

The world's winds have an amazingly simple engine—atmospheric pressure. Air has pressure, like water. But the pressure varies greatly from day to day and from place to place. Wherever there are differences in pressure, it makes the air move and generates winds, blowing from areas of high pressure to areas of low pressure.

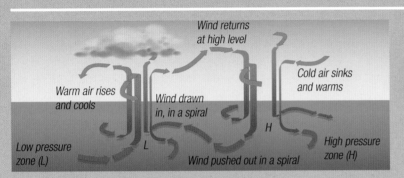

Wind returns at high level

Warm air rises and cools

Wind drawn in, in a spiral

Cold air sinks and warms

Low pressure zone (L)

Wind pushed out in a spiral

High pressure zone (H)

Wind driven

The sharper the pressure difference or "pressure gradient" between highs and lows, the stronger the wind it generates. But wind doesn't blow straight from high to low. Instead, it's steered off course by the way the Earth spins. So it spirals out of highs and into lows. This is why strong lows are called "cyclones" (cycling one way) and powerful highs are called "anticyclones" (cycling the other).

Why do winds bend

Winds never flow straight. Instead, they're spun by the Earth to the right in the northern hemisphere and to the left in the southern hemisphere. If they flow far enough, they curl right around in loops, clockwise in the north and counterclockwise in the south. This is called the "Coriolis effect."

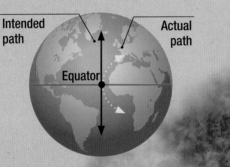

Intended path

Actual path

Equator

Isobars

You'll see pressure marked on weather maps as lines called "isobars." A bar is the basic unit of pressure, just marginally less than the average atmospheric pressure at ground level. The variations are slight, so they are measured in millibars (one thousandth of a bar). Isobars on the map run between places where the pressure in millibars is the same.

Warm front

Cold front

Isobar

Checking the pressure

In a room with no windows, how could you tell if you were on top of a mountain or deep under the ground? You could use a barometer, a device that measures atmospheric pressure. This decreases the higher you go, from 1.013 bars at sea level to around 0.3 bars on the top of Mount Everest! Easy!

The barometer was invented in 1643. Now, even smartphones have them!

Low pressure

Lows, or depressions, with their accompanying fronts, are the bringers of storms. Sometimes, lows are created when currents high up draw air upward. Other times, they're created when the Sun warms the ground more, making the air expand and rise. Rising air creates clouds and rain and sucks in winds. Once winds begin to spiral strongly into lows, they are cyclones, and can develop into powerful storms.

High pressure

High pressure zones, or anticyclones, are fine weather friends. When air sinks, it gets squeezed and warmed, like when you pump a bicycle tire really hard. So anticyclones give clear skies and fine weather. In the tropics, the effect of high pressure can be so strong that it creates deserts.

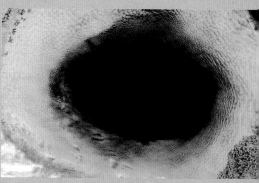

Standing firm

Low pressure zones create the mighty storms that often smash giant waves against Europe's Atlantic coast. Lighthouses, like this one in Portugal, are built to withstand the ocean, guiding ships through the dark, and warning them of danger. They have done so, standing firm against the weather, for a thousand years or more.

WIND PATTERNS

GLOBAL WEATHER MAKERS

Local winds spring up all the time. But all winds are part of a vast global machine that loops air from the cold poles to the warm equator, and back again. The Earth's spinning then twists it all into fantastic whirls, and in each hemisphere, the loop is broken into three great rolls, called cells. It's these cells that give us the major, prevailing winds that bring most of our windy weather.

Airplane in the wind

Above the edge of the Polar Cell—the cell that loops around the North Pole—there's a superfast wind high up. It's called the polar jet stream and whizzes right round the world from west to east. Airline pilots flying across the Atlantic know all about it and use it frequently to give a speed boost when flying eastward, "It's just like surfing," said one pilot. But it only works one way.

Circulation Cells

The atmosphere moves in giant, vertical loops called "cells," creating winds that blow from high pressure areas to lows and ground level, then high up again. The major global winds are generated by three major global cells: The Hadley Cell in the tropics, the Ferrel Cell in the temperate zone, and the Polar Cell in the polar zone. Air is moved north or south by the cell, but is also bent east or west by the Earth's spin. The ground-level part of each cell is the prevailing wind—the wind blowing most of the time—in each of three zones around the world.

Watching the weather

In 2018, the European Space Agency launched a satellite called *Aeolus*. It fires lasers at the atmosphere and detects the way they bounce back off particles of gas, dust, and moisture in the air. These particles move with the wind, so *Aeolus* can monitor changes in position and track global wind circulation continually for the first time.

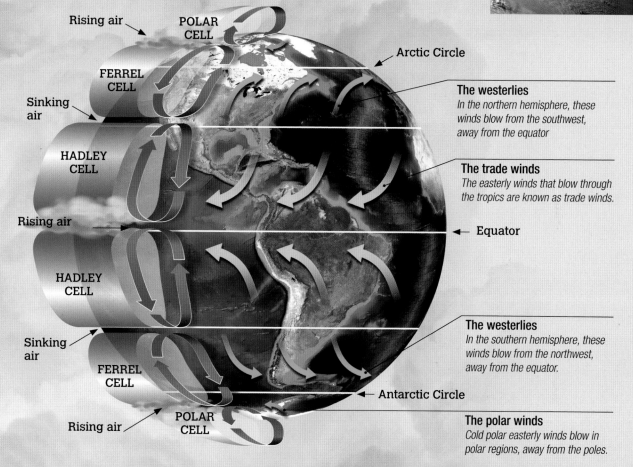

Rising air

POLAR CELL

FERREL CELL

Sinking air

HADLEY CELL

Rising air

HADLEY CELL

Sinking air

FERREL CELL

Rising air

POLAR CELL

Arctic Circle

The westerlies
In the northern hemisphere, these winds blow from the southwest, away from the equator

The trade winds
The easterly winds that blow through the tropics are known as trade winds.

Equator

The westerlies
In the southern hemisphere, these winds blow from the northwest, away from the equator.

Antarctic Circle

The polar winds
Cold polar easterly winds blow in polar regions, away from the poles.

Polar Cell

In the Polar Cell, chill air sinks at the poles and flows toward the polar front before looping back higher up. It is the lowest and weakest of the cells but creates bitter polar easterly winds (see p.45).

Ferrel Cell

This starts when air sinks in the subtropics and warms up. Some of this warm air joins the Hadley Cell as trade winds; the rest blows toward the Poles, creating warm, wet westerly winds, only to loop back as it meets polar air.

Hadley Cell

This is driven by strong Sun at the equator which makes warm air rise, and draws air in from the north and south. The rising air flows out at high level to the subtropics, sinks then loop backs at ground level as "trade winds."

TRADE WINDS

STRONG AIR CURRENTS

The tropics form a warm band around the world, located 1,860 miles (3,000 km) either side of the equator. Much of the weather here is shaped by the trade winds—steady winds that blow from the northeast or southeast, especially over oceans. Trade winds bring clear skies and a cool breeze to ease the tropical heat, but they can also bring mighty storms and scorching droughts.

Driving force

The trade winds are driven by the giant Hadley Cell. They begin in the subtropics in high pressure areas, and blow in toward the equator from north and south. They don't blow directly northward and southward because the spin of the Earth bends them more and more to the west as they move, so that they become northeasterly and southeasterly winds.

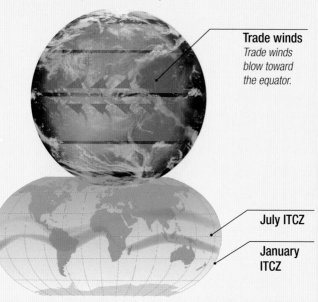

Trade winds
Trade winds blow toward the equator.

July ITCZ

January ITCZ

Meeting points

Trade winds from north and south meet along a wavy band around the world called the Intertropical Convergence Zone (ITCZ), "itch" for short. The ITCZ is where the sun heats the world most and drives a huge updraft of air that draws the trade winds in together. As the Sun migrates north and south through the year, it moves the ITCZ with it, with a dramatic impact on weather.

Florida orange

The skies above the southeast US are usually very clear. But some summers, trade winds pick up dust from the Sahara Desert and waft it across the Atlantic Ocean to Florida. The Saharan dust in the air creates fiery red sunsets in Florida. As our climate warms, and the desert expands, these dusty skies are becoming more common.

Stuck in the doldrums

Sailors have long been familiar with the ITCZ. But in the days of sail, they just knew it as the hellish zone where the wind stopped blowing. That's because all the air here is going directly up. So ships could get becalmed for days in the baking tropical heat. They called the ITCZ the "doldrums."

The sailor's wind

In the days of sail, trade winds gave ships their highways across the ocean on any westward journey. They pushed Christopher Columbus west across the Atlantic on his great voyage of discovery in 1492. To get back, he had to sail far north and find the damp, cold westerlies. The name "trade" actually comes from an old word for track, but the link with the trading ships of later centuries has stuck.

The "black pot"

Sailors also called the ITCZ the *pot au noir,* (the black pot) because the ferocious updrafts can create giant thunderclouds, or waterspouts.

Rain trees

Trade winds that blow across the ocean can pick up a lot of moisture and deliver deluges that create some of the wettest, warmest places on Earth—lush, tropical rain forests. But mysteriously, the rains in the Amazon rain forest start gently 2–3 months before the damp winds arrive. Scientists now think that the trees themselves release enough moisture into the air to create clouds and rain!

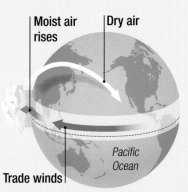

Moist air rises | Dry air

Pacific Ocean

Trade winds

Failing trade winds

In the Indian Ocean and southern Pacific, it's not Hadley Cells driving trade winds, it's Walker Cells. They circulate air east–west rather than north–south. In the Pacific, the winds pick up moisture from the ocean to dump vital rains on places like Indonesia, and drive an ocean current vital for marine life, the Walker current. But global warming is weakening this circulation, with worrying effects.

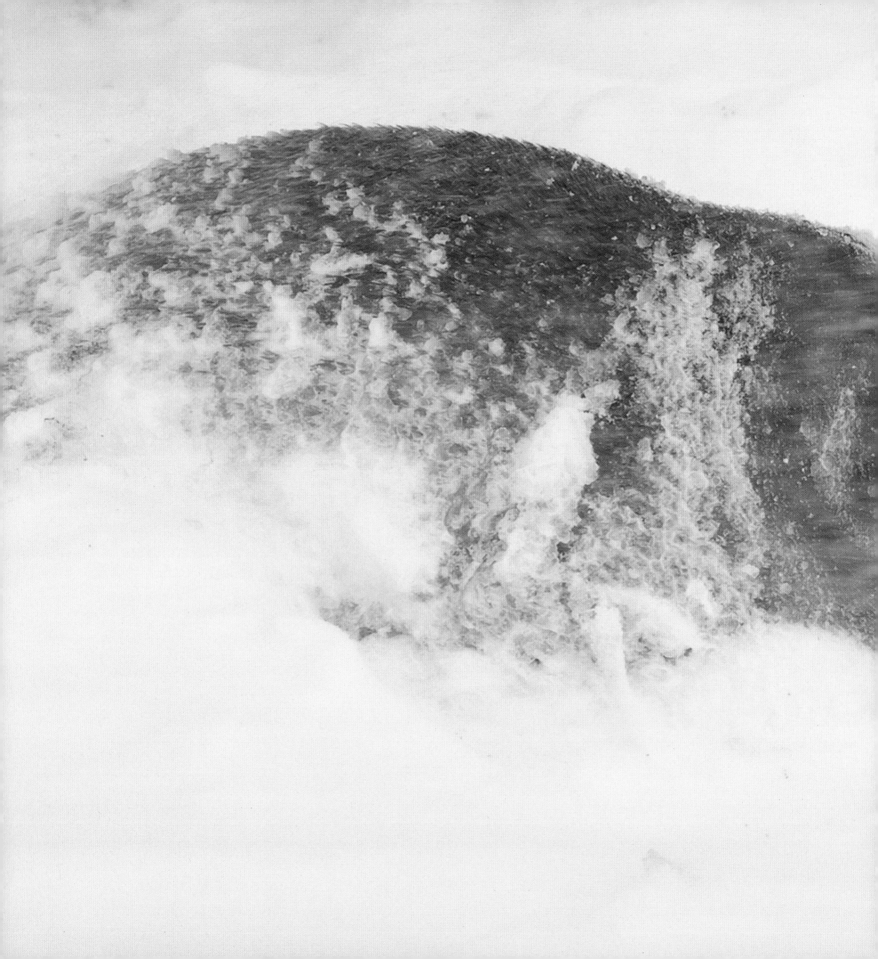

Penguins face-off polar easterlies

In polar regions, the prevailing winds here blow from the east. Known as polar easterlies, they are dry and often bitterly cold. Polar easterlies are born at the poles where the air is so chilly and dense it can only sink. This creates a high pressure zone that propels air outward toward the equator—southward from the North Pole and northward from the South Pole. The spinning of the Earth, and the Coriolis force, deflects these airflows ever farther eastward, creating the polar easterly winds.

In temperate regions, in winter, the shifting of the polar air masses allows these easterlies to blow in more often. If the weather vane shows the wind has swung around to the east, there's a high chance the weather will turn very chilly indeed as these polar winds inflict an icy blast. Occasionally, these easterlies can bring a massive dump of heavy snow as they clash with moister air. In Europe such wintry shocks have been dubbed "The Beast from the East." More often, though, easterlies bring clear, bright days in winter and icy nights. Rare summer appearances bring clear, dry weather, too.

WESTERLIES
STRONG WINDS

All through the year, but especially in late autumn and winter, westerly winds blow in over the ocean, battering western coasts in the midlatitudes with waves and gales, carrying rain-sodden clouds far over land. In the northern hemisphere, they come from the southwest. In the southern hemisphere, they come from the northwest.

Western blow

The westerly winds are driven by the giant Ferrel Cell which circulates air within the midlatitudes. They begin where air descends at the subtropics then blow away toward the poles. They don't blow directly northward and southward—the Earth's spin bends them to the east as they move, so that they become southwesterly, northwesterly, or westerly winds.

Westerlies
Westerly winds blow either side of the tropics, below each pole.

Rough seas
Strong winds whip up crashing waves that collide with this US Navy guided-missile cruiser in the Philippine Sea.

The Emerald Isle

Exposed to the westerlies coming off the Atlantic Ocean, western Ireland is wet. It gets about 45 inches (115 cm) of rain per year. This isn't much when compared to some tropical places, but barely a day goes by without some. People in Ireland talk of "soft" days—days when it might not rain, but there's damp mist or even drizzle in the air. All this moisture makes Ireland's grass very green, earning it the nickname the "Emerald Isle."

Green fields
Ireland's high rainfall gives the island many lush, green fields.

The horse latitudes

The zone where the westerlies start, about 30°N, are called the "horse latitudes." Here, air from both Hadley and Ferrell Cells descends, creating calm winds, sunny skies, and very little rain. According to legend, the name came from the days when many ships sailing to the Americas carried horses. Ships were often becalmed here and sometimes supplies of drinking water ran very low. When this happened, the sailors were sometimes forced to throw their horses overboard to save any water for themselves.

Atlantic storms

Although the heat of the tropics generates powerful hurricanes, the westerlies can stir up mighty storms, too. Like hurricanes, these storms form around spiralling areas of low pressure or depressions. The westerlies drive families of these extratropical cyclones against western coasts, bringing cool and cloudy weather, gales, and torrential rain, particularly in winter.

Location: 30-60° latitude in northern and southern hemispheres

Direction: From west to east and away from the equator

Cell: Ferrel Cell

Time: Strongest during the daytime

Season: Strongest during winter: December–February in northern hemisphere; June–August in southern hemisphere

Polar Front

Westerlies bring warm, wet air from the tropics crashing in to cold polar air along the Polar Front, which runs around the world about 60°N. It's here that the worst westerly storms begin. The Polar Front is the biggest single influence on weather across all of the US, except the deep south, plus Europe and Japan, too.

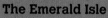

The Roaring Forties

In the southern hemisphere, westerly winds can hurtle uninterrupted over the ocean almost right around the world. They can blow so strong and fast that sailors named the zone between 40° and 50° the Roaring Forties. Sailors now know weather gets even worse south of 50°, dubbed the Furious Fifties and worse still south of 60°, the Screaming Sixties.

"Roaring Forties"

"Furious Fifties"

"Screaming Sixties"

"Rivers" in the air

At any given moment, there are three to five atmospheric "rivers" in each hemisphere, providing most of the world's north-to-south water vapor transport. The warmer the atmosphere, the more moisture they contain. When an atmospheric river reaches a coast, the "river" descends on the land as heavy rain or snow. These elongated corridors of concentrated moisture may be more than 1,000 miles (1,600 km) long, up to 620 miles (1,000 km) wide, and around 1.8 miles (3 km) deep.

ATMOSPHERIC RIVERS

WATER DELIVERY SYSTEMS

Picture a wide, fast-flowing river, such as the Mississippi or the Amazon, floating through the sky above your head. That is what an atmospheric river (AR) is—a broad band of water vapor carried from the tropics on strong winds such as the jet stream (see p. 30). When these "rivers in the sky" reach land, they bring storms that drop deluges of rain and snow on places such as California, the Pacific Northwest, and Alaska.

Roads made impassible by snow in the Sierra Nevada Mountains

Mudslide caused by flooding on the coast in Montecito, California

Benefits and dangers

Atmospheric rivers can be weak or strong. Weak ones provide many areas with much-needed rainfall and do no real harm. However, powerful ones, such as the "Pineapple Express" (see right), hold enormous amounts of water vapor and travel wi very strong winds, dumping rain or snow in such great quantities that they can bring flooding, mudslides, and avalanches.

Although the most frequent events occur over the western side of the Americas, ARs also impact other parts of world, resulting in chaos and risk to life.

The Moldau Castle above flooding in Prague, Czech Republic, in 2013

The basilica of Luján, near Buenos Aires, Argentina, during the floods of 2015

No rivers in the air, no rivers on land

The absence of an atmospheric river can be just as disastrous as its presence. California (above) is particularly sensitive to years in which it is not visited by an atmospheric river, because the "rivers" provide up to 50 percent of the water the state needs. For several years now, California has suffered from a prolonged and dangerous drought that has dried out creek beds and dropped little snow on its mountains. In mid-March 2019, a particularly strong atmospheric river delivered very heavy rain and snowfall, after which the state was declared drought-free.

Rain clouds above Cape Town, South Africa—around 70 percent of winter rainfall comes from ARs

tion (IMERG) February 15-21, 2017

9.4   12.6   15.7   18.9 Inches
240   320   400   480mm

The Pineapple Express

During winter, the atmospheric river known as the "Pineapple Express" typically brings heavy precipitation. Driven by a southern branch of the polar jet stream, his strong AR runs between Hawaii and the western coasts of the US and Canada. Bloated with water vapor, it sweeps in from the Pacific and up over he coastal mountains, shedding moisture in the form of rain as it goes. The river" then travels over the Central Plains and climbs up the western slopes f the Sierra Nevada Mountains, where it smothers the high ridges with snow.

Liuzhou, China, flooded by the Liujiang River, 23 ft (7.13 m) above the warning level, 2009

WINDY DAYS

Ancient sailors were at the mercy of the wind. Too little and their ships wouldn't go anywhere; too much made the sea treacherous. In 1805, Irish admiral Francis Beaufort introduced a scale to measure the different strengths of wind at sea, and this was later applied to winds on land. Today, the Beaufort scale is still used in some places, but wind speeds are usually measured with digital devices.

BEAUFORT SCALE

0

Calm

Wind speed: *less than 1 mph (less than 1.6 km/h)*
At sea: The surface of the sea is smooth, like a mirror.
On land: Smoke from a chimney or fire rises vertically.

1

Light air

Wind speed: *1–3 mph (1–5 km/h)*
At sea: Scale-like ripples move over the water's surface.
On land: Smoke drifts, indicating the wind direction.

2

Light breeze

Wind speed: 4–7 mph (6–11 km/h)
At sea: Small wavelets appear, but their glassy crests do not break.
On land: You can feel the wind on your face, and see it rustle leaves and move wind vanes.

3

Gentle breeze

Wind speed: *8–12 mph (12–19 km/h)*
At sea: The wavelets are larger, with crests that begin to break and scattered white, foamy caps.
On land: Light flags flutter, and leaves and small twigs are moved by the wind.

4

Moderate breeze

Wind speed: *13–18 mph (20–28 km/h)*
At sea: There are now small waves of up to 4 ft (1.2 m), and more whitecaps.
On land: The wind lifts dust and loose paper off the ground and moves small branches.

5

Fresh breeze

Wind speed: *19–24 mph (29–38 km/h)*
At sea: Waves take longer to form but are larger, up to 8 ft (2.4 m) high, many with whitecaps and some spray.
On land: Small trees in leaf begin to sway—it's good kite-flying weather.

6

Strong breeze

Wind speed: *25–31 mph (38–49 km/h)*
At sea: Some waves are now 13 ft (4 m) tall, and there are white foam crests everywhere, with lots of spray.
On land: Large branches are moved by the wind, it is difficult to keep an umbrella up.

Calm sea

A calm sea is ideal for swimming but watersports, such as sailing and surfing need a bit more wind.

How wind is measured on the Beaufort scale

The Beaufort scale relates the "force" of the wind (its speed) to the signs visible at sea and on land. So, it's not an absolute scale, it relies, to a certain extent, on how the observer interprets what they see. On the Beaufort scale, a calm, still day has a wind force of 0, and a hurricane rates as force 12.

"Hurricane" comes from "Huracan," an ancient Mayan wind god.

7	8	9	10	11	12
Near gale	**Gale**	**Strong gale**	**Storm**	**Violent storm**	**Hurricane**
Wind speed: *32–38 mph (50–61 km/h)*	**Wind speed:** *39–46 mph (62–74 km/h)*	**Wind speed:** *47–54 mph (75–88 km/h)*	**Wind speed:** *55–63 mph (89–102 km/h)*	**Wind speed:** *64–72 mph (103–117 km/h)*	**Wind speed:** *73+ mph (118+ km/h)*
At sea: The sea begins to heap up, with waves up to 19 ft (5.5 m) high; streaks of white foam blow off breakers. **On land:** The wind can move whole trees, and you can feel the wind resisting you when you walk toward it.	**At sea:** Longer, larger waves tower as high as 25 ft (7.5 m), with lots of foam and spray. **On land:** Twigs break off trees and it's hard to make any progress walking toward the wind.	**At sea:** The sea rolls with high waves of up to 32 ft (9.8 m), whose crests topple over. **On land:** Minor damage to buildings, with roof tiles and chimney pots blowing off.	**At sea:** Very high, churning waves up to 41 ft (12.5 m), with overhanging crests. The sea is white with foam and visibility is poor. **On land:** Trees are broken or uprooted, and there is structural damage to buildings.	**At sea:** Huge waves, some rising up to 52 ft (15.8 m), may obscure smaller ships from view. **On land:** Widespread damage and disruption.	**At sea:** Monster waves of over 45 ft (13.7 m) are the norm, endangering life at sea and on land. **On land:** Hurricanes can devastate coastal towns and cities (pp. 86–91).

Modern methods

Nowadays, meteorologists don't just rely on the Beaufort scale—they need hard data, not estimations. Instead, they use instruments called anemometers to measure wind speed and direction more precisely. The most commonly used types have a set of cups or propeller-like vanes that generate an electric current as they spin in the wind. The strength of the current shows the wind speed.

Solar-powered anemometer

Cup anemometer

Hand-held anemometer

The Rose of Saturn

The Cassini spacecraft took this amazing picture of the spinning vortex at Saturn's north pole. Dubbed "the Rose" by NASA, this is the massive eye of a hurricane that measures 1,250 miles (2,000 km) across—about 20 times larger than the eyes of the largest hurricanes on Earth. It swirls with cloud speeds of up to 330 mph (530 km/h).

WEATHER IN SPACE

To see really wild weather, you need to take a ride across our galaxy. You'd be blasted by dust storms on Mars, your bones would shatter in the ice of Neptune and Saturn, and the atmosphere on Venus is so thick that heat barely escapes and you'd be cooked in seconds. And it's probably best to avoid the massive storms in the depths of space where turbulent gases mix violently and young stars are born.

The center of a storm in a star-forming cloud, NGC 3603

A raging storm on Saturn

Storms in outer space

Storms on Earth may be devastating, but there are some monster hurricanes on Jupiter and Saturn. Spectacular gas storms rage in far constellations and signal the birth of stars, while cosmic dust storms tell us when they die.

Seasonal variations

Mars, like Earth, has polar ice caps and seasons, but its atmosphere is mostly carbon dioxide and temperatures may drop to –225°F (–153°C) at the poles. The Martian year is almost twice as long as an Earth year, and spring is its longest season. Uranus has seasons as well, but a Uranus year is 84 Earth-years long, and each season lasts 21 years.

Sunset on Mars

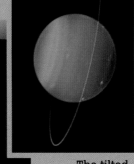

The tilted planet Uranus

Enceladus, a moon of Saturn

Neptune's moon Triton

Frozen worlds

The gas giant Neptune's atmosphere, with its mix of hydrogen, helium, and methane, has the highest winds of any planet and a surface temperature of –330°F (–201°C). One of its moons, Triton, with its crust of frozen nitrogen, is even colder at –390°F (–235°C). Saturn's moon Enceladus's icy surface is a bright white crust, beneath which lies an ocean of liquid salty water, from which jets of icy particles spew far out into space.

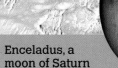

In 2018, a global dust storm engulfed most of the surface of Mars, the red planet.

Heat

Venus is by far the hottest planet in our solar system, with temperatures of more than 880°F (470°C). Its atmosphere is made up mainly of carbon dioxide, and its sulfuric acid clouds act as a blanket, causing a runaway greenhouse effect (see p. 22).

Coronal rain

It "rains" on the Sun, but it's not water. Superheated plasma—electrified gas—rises up from the Sun's surface in a magnetic loop, and falls back down in an arc. The plasma cools as it moves away from the surface and drips from the magnetic loop as coronal rain.

Small magnetic loop with coronal rain

Venus's sulfuric acid clouds

Clouds swirl around Venus

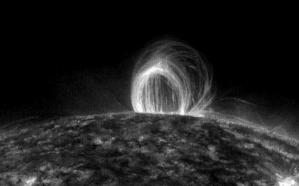

AMAZING

EVERY DAY

HOW CLOUDS FORM

RIDING THE WIND

Even on the sunniest days, there are usually a few wispy clouds in the sky. On other days, thick gray clouds can block out the Sun. Every cloud is just a mass of water droplets and ice crystals, so tiny and light that they float on the air. But no cloud is quite the same as another, and they're changing all the time. Some clouds just bring shade, others bring rain, snow, or even thunder and lightning.

Getting a lift

Clouds usually form when air rises. That is why clouds are mostly up in the sky, though they can form at ground level, too, under certain conditions. Because pressure drops with height, air expands as it rises and cools. When the air is saturated and cannot hold any more water vapor—it reaches its dew point—the moisture condenses into droplets, or else, if it is really cold, freezes directly to ice.

Warm air rising and cooling so clouds form

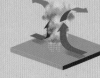

Warmth rising

Fluffy cumulus clouds can bring afternoon showers on summer days. These form when bubbles of warm, moist air appear above sun-baked patches on the ground. Lighter than the air around, the bubbles drift up as thermals, expanding and cooling as they rise. Eventually the droplets condense to form a cumulus cloud. Condensation releases heat, warming the air so it rises again to pile up the cloud.

Convergence lifting to give layers of clouds

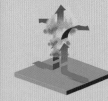

Push-ups!

When winds meet head on, this can create clouds. As they converge, there is nowhere for some of the air to go but up. This is called "convergence lifting." It often happens over a vast area and creates persistent layers of cloud.

Air driven upwards over high ground

Hill climbing

When moist air meets a mountain range, it often has no choice but to go up and over. As the air pushes on up the mountain slope it cools to its dew point and makes "orographic" clouds and often rain. Up in the High Sierras of California people rely on rain falling like this for their water supply.

Warm, moist air rising over cold air at a front

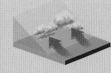

Wedge-up

When two air masses come together along a front, uplift and clouds are inevitable. It may be that the cold air wedges itself under the warm air along a cold front, and shoves the warm air up sharply, or the warm air slides gradually up over the cold at a warm front. It always results in moist air rising and clouds forming.

Stable air

Air always cools at much the same rate as it rises, but the conditions in the air into which it rises can vary. If a rising air bubble is cooler than the surrounding air, it will tend to sink, stopping cloud build-up. Air that tends to sink is called "stable air." If it is warmer, it is unstable and goes on rising and cloud-building (below.) But even stable air can be forced to rise by a hill or front. If so, the cloud spreads out sideways as stratus (layer) clouds.

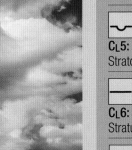

Cloud classification

Nowadays, clouds are always known by Latin words such as *cumulus* and *stratus*. In 1802, a 30-year-old Quaker named Luke Howard found a way to put all the myriad, ever-changing clouds in the sky into simple groups. He classified them according to their shape—cumulus (heaped), stratus (flattened), cirrus (curly i.e. wispy); their height—alto (medium height); and raininess—nimbus (rain cloud). There are 27 cloud states and they have all been assigned a unique international letter and number classification that is used by meteorologists as a form of shorthand when they are making weather reports.

LOW CLOUDS

 C_L1: Cumulus

 C_L2: Cumulus

 C_L3: Cumulonimbus

 C_L4: Stratocumulus

 C_L5: Stratocumulus

 C_L6: Stratus

 C_L7: Stratus fractus

 C_L8: Cumulus and stratocumulus

 C_L9: Cumulonimbus

MEDIUM CLOUDS

 C_M1: Altostratus

 C_M2: Altostratus or nimbostratus

 C_M3: Altocumulus

 C_M4: Altocumulus

 C_M5: Altocumulus

 C_M6: Altocumulus

 C_M7: Altocumulus

 C_M8: Altocumulus

 C_M9: Altocumulus

HIGH CLOUDS

 C_H1: Cirrus

 C_H2: Cirrus

 C_H3: Cirrus

 C_H4: Cirrus

 C_H5: Cirrostratus

 C_H6: Cirrostratus

 C_H7: Cirrostratus

 C_H8: Cirrostratus

 C_H9: Cirrocumulus

LOW-LEVEL CLOUDS

ALL-WEATHER CLOUDS

Cumulonimbus, the great thunderhead clouds (see pp. 98–99), can tower more than 75,000 ft (23,000 m), reaching right up into the stratosphere, higher than any other cloud. But these massive clouds are still classified as low-level clouds. It is the base height that matters, and even towering cumulonimbus clouds start below 6,500 ft (around 2,000 m) above the ground, so are classed as low-level clouds.

How low do clouds form?
In fact, clouds can form right down to the ground. However, those that form at ground level are usually thought of as fog.

CUMULUS HUMILIS

C11 FAIRWEATHER CLOUDS

Cumulus clouds are the fluffy clouds built up by thermals on a sunny day, often floating through the blue sky entirely by themselves. Their tops shine brilliant white in the Sun, but their bases are often in dark shadow. The tops look like cauliflower florets, but the base can be flat.

Fairweather clouds
Cumulus are often called "fairweather clouds," particularly if they develop from rather shapeless cumulus fractus into the more defined cumulus humilis.

Blanket of cloud
These clouds can stretch across the entire sky and cover the tops of tall buildings or hills. They can bring light drizzle but never rain.

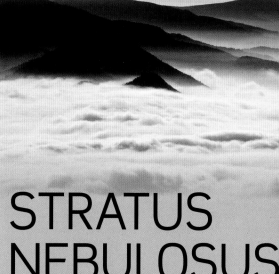

STRATUS NEBULOSUS

C16 BLANKETING CLOUD

Stratus nebulosus are the most shapeless clouds of all. They are just one vast, blank, damp mass lying across the sky. They do not come from rising air currents. Instead, they form when cool, very moist breezes blow gently over a cold sea or land, triggering condensation below 1,600 ft (500 m), close to the ground.

CUMULUS CONGESTUS

C12 TOWERING CUMULUS

As moisture condenses, it releases heat. The heat can warm up the cloud. Cells of rising air develop inside the cloud, sending cloud plumes billowing up and making the cloud higher and thicker. The result? Cumulus congestus, which may bring with it rain showers.

Traveling upward
Over the course of a full day, these clouds can pile high before the cool of evening stops the updraft. In the tropics, they bring heavy rain later in the day.

STRATOCUMULUS STRATIFORMIS

C15 HORIZONTAL LAYERS

Stratocumulus are the most common clouds in the sky. They have slightly fluffy shapes, and they are formed by the lifting or breakup of fine clouds. They form in dark rolls or patches, often with blue sky between.

Dramatic colors at sunset

Most common
These clouds block out a lot of sunlight, which is why they are dark,. They can look quite dramatic when rays break through, but they rarely produce much rain.

Blown along
Carried by a strong breeze, these clouds often appear to be rain clouds themselves, but any rain is actually falling from denser clouds above, not from the stratus.

STRATUS FRACTUS

CL7 SCUDDING CLOUDS

Often known as "scud" clouds, these rags of clouds often whisk in ahead of rain carried by bigger, thicker nimbostratus clouds.

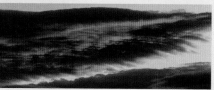

STRATOCUMULUS CASTELLANUS

C15 TURRETED CLOUDS

Height of base: 1,200–6,500 ft (365–2,000 m)

Shape: cumuliform "lump" at base

Latin: *stratus*—flattened; *cumulus*—heap

Precipitation: light

Castles in the air
The crenellated appearance is most obvious when the cloud is seen from the side. These clouds are sometimes taller than they are wide.

Sometimes, if there is a fair amount of rising warm air, rolls of stratocumulus can pile up in towers, known as stratocumulus castellanus, which have a crenellated (castle battlement) appearance. If they go on piling up, they can turn into cumulus congestus or cumulonimbus.

MID-LEVEL CLOUDS

ICE CRYSTALS AND WATER DROPLETS

Above 6,500 ft (2,000 m) the mid-level clouds are the "alto" clouds along with nimbostratus. They look more distant than low-level clouds and that is not just because they are higher, but also because they are thinner and wispier. It is cold this high—from freezing down to −13°F (−25°C) in midlatitudes—and they are filled with ice crystals as well as water droplets. Even the water droplets are tiny and supercooled, staying liquid well below freezing.

In search of a name
Sometimes the sky is such a mess of clouds, it is hard to identify exactly what the clouds are. That is where the classification "altocumulus of a chaotic sky" comes in. This describes a riot of clouds that are broken into patches and sheets at all heights, and a sky that has a heavy, stagnant look.

Veiled sunlight
Altostratus are veils of cloud that spread right across the sky, creating dull, overcast weather. The Sun may peep palely through, but the clouds are too thick to create halos like the higher cirrostratus.

ALTOSTRATUS TRANSLUCIDUS

Cm1 CLOUDY SKIES

Altostratus can form from descending cirrostratus or spreading cumulonimbus, but mostly they are created by the uplift of large masses of air on a warm or occluded front. At warm fronts, they can thicken into nimbostratus. If so, you can be sure that rain is on its way.

NIMBOSTRATUS

Cm2 LOW-HANGING CLOUDS

Nimbostratus is the ultimate gloomy-day cloud. It spreads its dark gray mass right across the sky, blocking out the Sun. Sometimes it is so dark, you need to turn the lights on! What is worse, it often brings light rain or snow, long, cold, and relentless.

ALTOCUMULUS

Cm3 PATCHES IN THE SKY

Height of base: 6,500 ft (2,000 m)

Shape: white or gray rounded lumps dotted across the sky, smaller and more compact than stratocumulus

Latin: *altus*—high; *cumulus*—heaped

Precipitation: rare; even if it falls it doesn't reach the ground

Altocumulus are rather patchy clouds, but they have a more definite shape than cirrostratus, because they contain water droplets as well as ice. They often form from the slow break-up of altostratus and can indicate the coming of a cold front. They can be mistaken for cirrocumulus, but if they have any gray, they're definitely altocumulus.

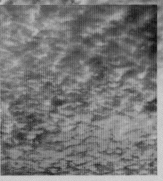

Drama in the sky
These dramatic clouds are the most likely to create tricks of the light (see pp. 80-81).

Height of base: below 8,500 ft (3,000 m); 6,500 ft (2000 m) in Antarctica

Shape: big, flat cloud blanket

Latin: *nimbus*—rain; *stratus*—flattened

Precipitation: light to moderate

Dark days
Often nimbostratus just will not go away, hanging about for hours. After a time, shreds of pannus cloud or scuds can develop underneath.

Heralding rain
If you see these cloudlets in the evening, the dawn is likely to bring rain, especially if the rising sun is warm enough to stir up cumulus clouds and bring them into the mix.

ALTOCUMULUS FLOCCUS

Cm8 RAGGED CLOUDLETS

In warm, unstable conditions, altocumulus can break up into little cloudlets, like row upon row of balls of fluff, called altocumulus floccus. The lower parts of these are usually ragged. The clouds can sometimes pile up into the crenellated castle shape of altocumulus castellanus.

HIGH-LEVEL CLOUDS

ICE CRYSTAL CLOUDS

High, high in the sky in the mid-latitudes it gets very cold indeed! That is why high-level clouds—clouds over 3 miles (5 km) up in the atmosphere—are all made of ice crystals. That is also why they are wispy and thin, and are given the general name cirrus, from the Latin word for a "curl of hair." In the tropics, the air rarely gets this cold until well over 4 miles (7 km) up, so you will see these clouds much more rarely in those regions.

Height of base: 20,000 ft (6,000 m)

Shape: relatively flat layers or patches

Latin: *cirrus*—curl of hair; *cumulus*—heap; *stratiformis*—spread out

Precipitation: none

CIRRUS UNCINUS

Ch1 HAIR-LIKE CLOUDS

Beautiful, wispy cirrus are the highest common clouds, forming over 4 miles (7 km) up. They are also the fastest moving. Famous folk singer Joni Mitchell sang of them as "flows of angel hair," and they are commonly known as "mares' tails." They are, in a way, distant snow because they are made of ice crystals that are falling from fast-moving air above, then trailing behind.

Due warning
These clouds are the cloud whisperers that quietly warn that a warm front and rough weather are on the way.

Cloud sequence
In the northern hemisphere, if you stand with your back to the wind and the clouds spread out to your right, you can be pretty sure the cirrus will thicken into cirrostratus, the cirrostratus will grow into altrostratus, and the altostratus into nimbostratus.

CIRRUS UNCINUS

Ch4 SPREADING CLOUDS

Meteorologists know just what to expect if cirrus clouds spread and fill the sky. In fact, the long name of this formation, cirrus uncinus—progressively invading the sky, is part of a familiar cloud sequence (see above) which leads to a warm front and lots of hard rain.

CIRRUS SPISSATUS

Ch2 DENSEST OF ALL

Cirrus spissatus are the thickest of all the cirrus clouds. They can be so thick that they even appear gray. They are typically the remnants of the anvil of a thundercloud, left hanging after the storm has blown itself out.

Good times
Fair weather will persist as long as they appear in patches, but these clouds may partly o completely obscure the Sun.

CIRROCUMULUS STRATIFORMIS

Ch9 STORM WARNING

Cirrocumulus form dappled patterns of small ripples high in the sky. They can look even more like fish scales than the "mackerel skies" of altocumulus clouds, which are formed at a lower level. Cirrocumulus are generally a sign that bad weather is on the way. First, this much moisture high up suggests the air is unstable. Second, the ripples indicate that high-level winds are whipping along—a sign that a big storm is coming.

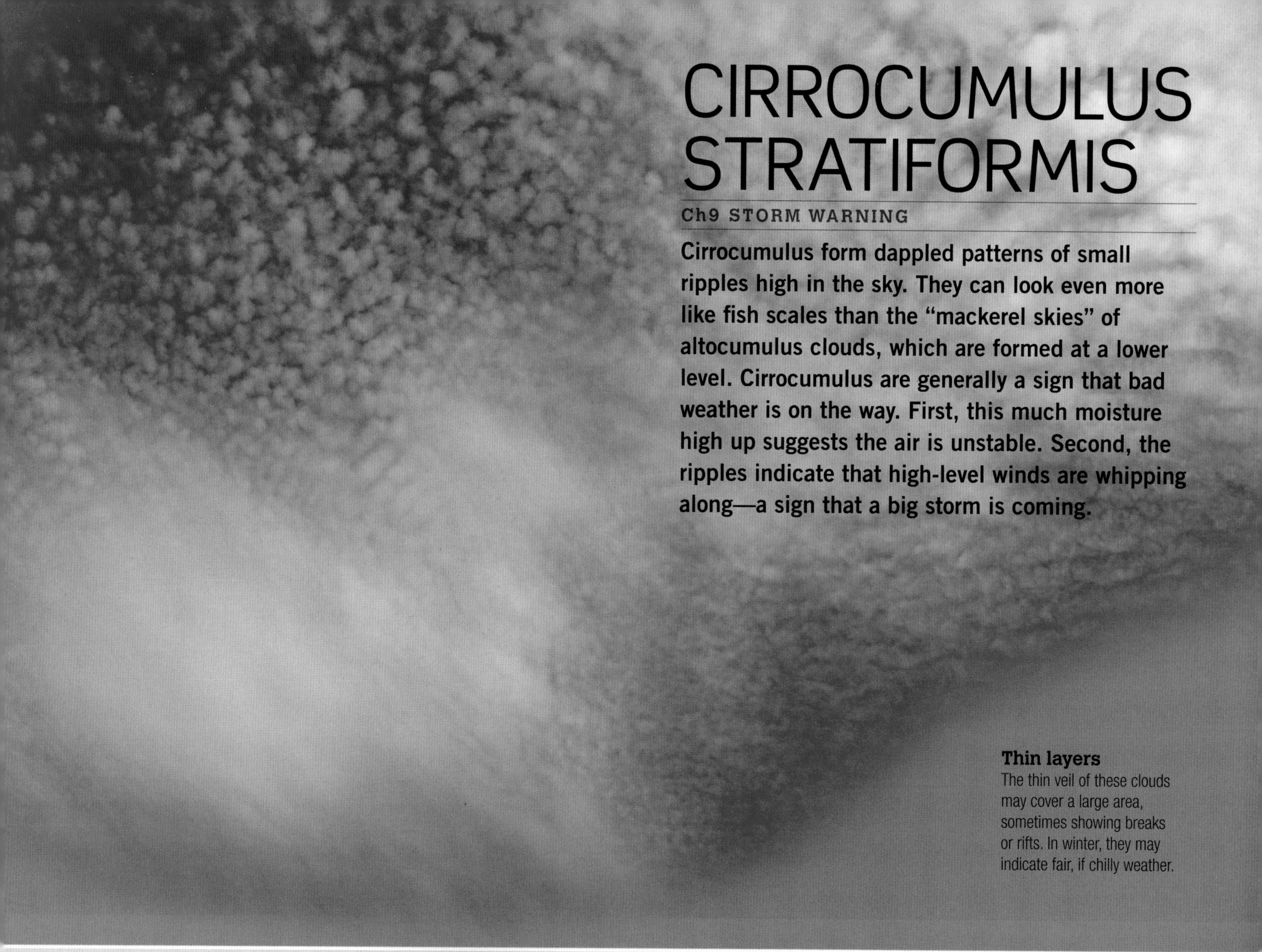

Thin layers
The thin veil of these clouds may cover a large area, sometimes showing breaks or rifts. In winter, they may indicate fair, if chilly weather.

CIRROSTRATUS

Ch6 SHEETLIKE HIGH CLOUDS

Cirrostratus are delicate veils of thin, widespread ice crystals. These clouds are rather thicker than cirrus, from which they often develop, and they cover more of the sky, so that the Sun and Moon are often seen haloed through them. Some cirrostratus have a wavelike appearance.

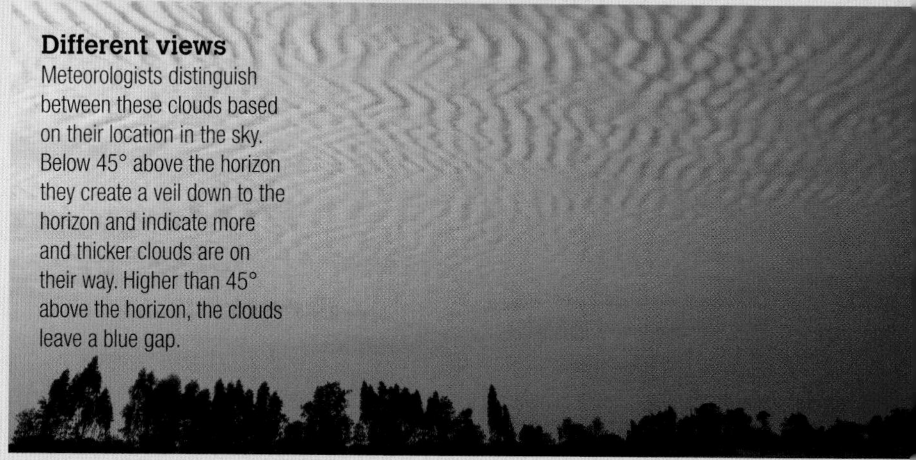

Different views
Meteorologists distinguish between these clouds based on their location in the sky. Below 45° above the horizon they create a veil down to the horizon and indicate more and thicker clouds are on their way. Higher than 45° above the horizon, the clouds leave a blue gap.

RARE CLOUDS

SHOWTIME IN THE SKY

Even if you are familiar with the "regular" cloud types, you may still spot some rare and unusual clouds. In the right conditions, some weird and wonderful cloud shapes form, including ocean-like ripples, dangling pouches, and long, rolling cloud banks that resemble huge breaking waves that look good enough to surf!

High-level trails
Contrails usually occur above 20,000 ft (6,000 m).

Contrails
Maybe not rare, but certainly special, these white streaks are all that are left when water vapor from aircraft exhausts condenses and freezes. Some long-lasting contrails may transform into cirrus clouds.

Cloud on cloud
Here a pileus cloud has formed over the ash cloud from an eruption of Sarychev Peak, a stratovolcano on Matua Island, one of the Kuril Islands, Russia. The scene was captured by astronauts on the International Space Station in June 2009.

Height: above 6,500 ft (2,000 m), although usually much higher

Shape: smooth and covering the top of a towering cloud like an umbrella

When seen: when a cloud is growing quickly and indicating that a thunderstorm may be on the way

PILEUS

A CLOUD-SPOTTER'S FAVORITE

Also called the scarf or cap cloud, this uncommon thin sheet of cloud usually perches above a cumulus or cumulonimbus cloud, like a hat on someone's head. Made of ice crystals, it may reflect rainbow-like colors.

Height: below 6,500 ft (2,000 m)

Shape: low-level, horizontal tube-shaped or shelf-like in appearance with motion in the leading edge and turbulent underside—may last only a short period of time

When seen: during spring and summer when thunderstorms are common

ARCUS

LEADING THE WAY

Seen at the leading edge of thunderstorms, these roll or shelf-shaped clouds can herald anything from a strong, windy cold front to a supercell thunderstorm (see pp. 104–105) that carries with it a severe weather warning.

Low roller
This spectacular roll cloud has been created by cooler winds inside the storm colliding with warmer air.

Swirling stunner
This photograph of asperitas above Hanmer Springs, South Island, New Zealand shows the cloud at its most dramatic.

ASPERITAS

NEW ON THE BLOCK

This spectacular cloud formation was only categorized by meteorologists in 2015. The name comes from the Latin *aspero*, meaning "to make rough," and the appearance is certainly that of rippling waves in a rough sea.

Height: below 6,500 ft (2,000 m) when stratocumulus; 6,500–20,000 ft (2,000–6,100 m) when altocumulus

Shape: wavy undersurface caused by the wind direction changing with height

When seen: often in the morning through midday after thunderstorms

MAMMATUS
HARBINGERS OF BAD WEATHER

These clouds are a rare example of clouds formed by sinking air. When cold, saturated air from high up in the atmosphere becomes heavier than the air around it, it sinks back toward the ground. It eventually appears in rounded shapes below the cloud base—often the underside of cumulonimbus (see pp. 98–99).

Height: above 30,000 ft (9,000 m) when associated with a cumulonimbus anvil

Shape: pouches, hanging from the undersides of the cloud base, usually the anvil of cumulonimbus

When seen: usually after the worst of a thunderstorm has passed

Dangerous beauty
Illuminated at sunset, bubbly mammatus clouds, composed of ice and water, are a magnificent sight. They are associated with severe weather, appearing before, during, or after a storm. A single pouch can range up to 5 miles (8 km) across and a cloud of mammatus may extend for dozens of miles in all directions. They dissipate when the cloud droplets and ice crystals that form them evaporate.

Dark and stormy mammatus

Uneven and opaque mammatus

Neat rows of mammatus

Varied in appearance
The pouches of mammatus are most visible when they are framed by sunlight. They may be smooth or ragged, opaque or translucent, in serried ranks or scattered across the sky in different sizes, and may last for ten minutes or several hours.

Low clouds

Most of the time, air gets colder higher up. That's why mountain tops are chilly and clouds form high in the sky. But occasionally, this pattern reverses in the lowest layer of the atmosphere, near the ground. In fact, up to a certain height, the temperature climbs. Effectively, a slab of warm air is sitting on top of a slab of cool air, which sits on the ground. This unusual arrangement is called a "temperature inversion."

A temperature inversion acts like a lid, trapping air near the ground. Of course, it's not just air that is trapped but moisture, too, and in big cities like Shanghai, China, and Los Angeles, California, urban pollution gets mixed in to create a thick soup. With a soup like this, it's no wonder low-level clouds form, and spread out in layers below the inversion ceiling. The problem is made worse by urban development, which cuts down air circulation, blocking off through drafts, while traffic and everyday city business spew dust and other pollution into the air. The inversion is often so low that the tallest buildings (as seen here in Shanghai) emerge into the clear air above it like mysterious islands above a fluffy gray sea.

RAINFALL RECORDS

Most rain in 1 minute:
1.23 in (31.2 mm) on July 4, 1956, at Unionville, Maryland

Most rain in a year:
1,042 in (26,470 mm), Cohra, India, 1860–61

Most consecutive days with rain: 331 days, Oahu, Hawaii, 1939–40

Highest average annual rainfall:
467.4 in (11,872 mm) Mawsynram, India

Wettest country:
Colombia averages 127.6 in (3,240 mm) of rain per year

Least rainy place:
Antarctica's Dry Valleys, which have seen no rain for 2 million years

RAIN

A single, big cloud can hold more than 550 tons (0.5 million kg) of water—that's about one-fifth of the water in an Olympic-sized swimming pool! Yet it will all stay floating in the sky overhead . . . until it starts to rain. Then down comes a lot of the water—teeming down in just a few minutes from the tallest cumulonimbus and cumulus clouds, or falling steadily over many hours from shallower nimbostratus.

Think raindrops are tear-shaped? Think again! They're spherical or button-shaped.

The big drop
Raindrops grow bigger in two ways. In warm clouds, they join up or smash together (coalescence and convergence In cold clouds, or cold parts of clouds, growing ice crystal join water droplets and become snow.

Rain starters
Cloud droplets are one-millionth the size of raindrops. So something has to kickstart the process of making them grow. As in the original formation of the cloud, the trigger is uplift: The cloud must be lifted and cooled so that the air gets saturated and releases more water. Three typical methods of uplift are thermals, mountains, and fronts.

Falling rain
Rain is by far the most common kind of precipitation. In the tropics, it's really the only kind. Drops range from a fraction of an inch (drizzle) to more than 0.2 inches (5 mm). Small drops are spherical. Large drops are actually like fat buttons.

Warm clouds

...all begins when saturated air is swept up, cools, ...nd condenses. As droplets are carried aloft, ...ey meet newly condensing drops and grow ...ntil they're too heavy to float on the air. ...hey then fall steeply, smashing into ...her rising droplets and swelling ...to raindrops. Sometimes, ...ey grow so big they split ...to more raindrops.

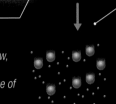

Raindrops

Cloud droplets

Updraft

Large drops

Getting bigger
The droplets get bigger as they bash into each other and clump together.

Going up
Saturated air rises rapidly in the updraft. It cools, causing condensation and forming water droplets in the clouds.

Moving down
Water droplets get heavier as they grow, until their weight overcomes the force of the updraft.

Falling rain
Large drops break up, but then grow again as they merge with other drops.

Ice crystals grow as they collect molecules from supercooled water droplets.

Water droplets shrink away, leaving only ice crystals.

Cold clouds

In cold clouds, rain may start as snow and only melt into rain as it falls through warmer air. Cold clouds are a mix of ice crystals and supercooled water droplets. The supercooled droplets lose vapor and shrink, providing water vapor that makes the ice crystals grow. When an ice crystal strikes a supercooled droplet, the water freezes, adding to the crystal. Ice crystals become snowflakes and start to fall.

Precipitation

It's not only rain that falls from clouds: It can also be drizzle, snow, hail, or sleet. Meteorologists call everything that falls from clouds "precipitation." Here are types of precipitation other than rain.

Sleet: A mixture of rain and snow that forms when some falling snow melts.

Snow: Snowflakes are ice crystals that grow as they fall through a cloud.

Hail: Large balls of ice that form in thunderclouds, building up layer by layer.

Graupel: Ice pellets form as supercooled snow droplets freeze onto ice crystals.

Freezing rain: This is supercooled raindrops that freeze on impact.

SNOW

FLAKES OF FROZEN FUN

Brr! The winter air is cold and the wind is in the right direction—so it could be snow time! Believe it or not, there's nearly always snow somewhere above you in the clouds in the midlatitudes. But if those clouds are going to dump crisp, white snow not soggy rain, the air needs to be colder than 35.6°F (2°C); otherwise, it just melts to mush on the way down. That's actually rare outside polar and mountain regions.

Dry snow

The most sparkling white snow is dry snow. This is the powder snow that skiers love. It forms when snow falls through dry, cold air, so that the snowflakes stay small, hard, and separate. It tends to fall quite fast and straight. When it lands, this kind of snow doesn't stick together, so it drifts and sprays if the weather is windy. It is no good for making snowballs!

Wet snow

Wet snow is snow falling through air that is slightly warmer than zero. So the edges of the snowflakes melt and other snowflakes stick to them. Wet snow forms big flakes that flutter slowly down. This is the kind of snow that lies thick and soft if the ground is cold—and it's ideal for snowball fights and building snowmen

Snowbringers

Most snow in the midlatitudes comes from the same cyclones that bring plentiful rain in the fall. These cyclones can be snowbringers in winter, because the air beneath the clouds is much colder, especially beneath a cold front. Snow can come with various different air masses (see pp. 32–33). In North America, the main culprits are polar maritime and polar continental air masses, which bring snow along the polar front.

Snowflakes

Tiny, six-sided, rod-shaped ice crystals link up to form flakes of snow. Scientists have identified 80 different kinds of snowflake.

Fernlike dendrites: very large star-shaped flakes with branches like ferns

Stellar dendrites: large branching flakes that form below −4°F (−20°C)

Thin plates: warmer, drier air leads to short, blunt, or non-existent arms

Simple prisms: single, almost microscopically small, six-sided crystals

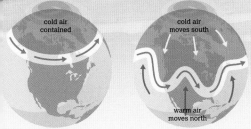

Polar vortex

When you hear on the news that the polar vortex is on the move, it's not some science-fiction horror! But it does mean that some frighteningly cold weather might be on the way. The vortex is a giant spiral of air that flows counterclockwise around the North Pole and helps to keep cold air close to the pole. It is completely encircled by a powerful river of air, or jet stream, highup. In some winters, the jet stream develops giant meanders and moves south, allowing the vortex to expand and bring icy weather to North America and Europe.

cold air contained

cold air moves south

warm air moves north

Snow line

Because it gets colder higher up, some mountaintops are permanently covered in snow, while their lower slopes remain snow-free. The division between the snowy bit and the snow-free bit is called the snow line, and it's often very marked. It varies with both the season and location. The snowline is highest at the tropics (over 16,400 ft / 5,000 m) and gets lower as you move toward the poles. Once you're in the polar circle, the snow line is at ground level.

SNOW RECORDS

Largest known snowflake:
15 in (38 cm) in diameter; it fell in January 1887 in Montana

Snowiest inhabited place:
Sukayu Onsen in Japan—57.87 ft (17.64 m) of snow per year.

Biggest snowfall in a 24-hour period: 8.4 ft (2.56 m) at Capracotta, Italy, in March 2015

Deepest snow recorded:
38.8 ft (11.82 m) on Mount Ibuki, Japan, in February 2013

Tallest snowperson: Olympia the snow-woman, built at Bethel, Maine, in February 2008, was a staggering 122 ft (37.2 m) tall

Jack Frost
Old folk stories tell of Jack Frost, who creeps up and paints patterns on windows, or nips noses and fingers with frostbite. His origins are unclear, but in Scandanavian tradition, he is the son of Kari, Norse god of the winds, while in Finnish folklore, Frostman and Frostwoman control the weather.

FROST
CRYSTAL PATTERNING

On still, clear, chilly nights, the ground can lose heat rapidly. As the ground cools, it cools the air above. As the air cools, moisture condenses on the cold ground as drops of dew, which often burn off quickly in the morning sun. But if the ground gets icy cold, the moisture freezes, coating surfaces with frost—leaves and branches as well as the ground. Frost can kill crops, which is one of the reasons people grow fruits and vegetables in greenhouses!

Dew
You can get dew in the morning almost anywhere in the world after a chilly, still night, even in the desert. It forms when moisture in the air cools to the point where it's saturated (see p. 20), called the dew point. Dew drops typically cover surfaces that cool off quickest, such as grass and leaves and car roofs.

Dew on grass

Single blade of grass with dew drop

Hoarfrost
Hoarfrost forms when moisture freezes directly without condensing first, creating tiny glistening white needles or spicules of ice. It gets its name from an old word for "ancient," because the spikes of ice look like bristles in an old man's beard. Late autumn and early spring, when there is lots of moisture in the air is the best time for hoarfrost.

Window frost
Frost can grow on the inside of windows as moisture in the room freezes on the cold glass. As with hoarfrost, the moisture freezes directly into ice crystals, creating beautiful patterns like fern fronds, This is why it's also called fern frost. But window frost is rare now that houses are double-glazed.

Rime
If the air is wet, moisture condenses first, then freezes like glass, covering twigs like a popsicle. When a very chilly wet wind blows, and the moisture becomes supercooled (see p. 69), it can coat surfaces with thick ice called rime, especially on the windward side.

Frost quake
A sudden freezing can put enormous stress on the ground and soil. In some instances, the stress is so great that it can even cause cryoseism, or a frost quake, in this instance cracking a solid granite rock in half.

Frost hollows
The most likely places for frost are low-lying areas—such as small valleys where dense, cold air drains from the hills during still, cold nights. Pockets like these where frost often forms are called "frost hollows".

Cold air
Cold air flows down the slopes and pools in the valley.

FOG AND MIST

LOW-HANGING CLOUDS

Not all clouds scud across the sky—some touch the ground. We call these clouds fog and mist. A dense, ground-level cloud that reduces visibility to less than 3,000 ft (1,000 m) is called fog; less dense clouds are called mist. Thick fog can be a big risk to road traffic, ships at sea, and low-flying aircraft, especially at landing or takeoff.

Morning mist

Mist may form over low ground after a clear night. Like all clouds, mist consists of suspended water droplets. If not carried off by a breeze, it soon disappears as the Sun's warmth turns the droplets back to vapor.

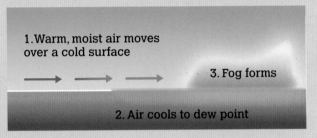

1. Warm, moist air moves over a cold surface

3. Fog forms

2. Air cools to dew point

Sideways air

The horizontal movement of air is called "advection," and it sometimes causes fog. When a warm, moist light wind blows over a cool surface, the air cools rapidly to its dew point, forming dense clouds of water droplets called "advection fog." This type of fog is common at sea or near the coast, but may also occur over land, especially in winter, when warm air blows over frozen or snow-covered ground. Typical advection fogs reach heights of up to a few hundred feet and can also occur with radiation fogs.

Victorian Londoners make their way through smog

Smoke + fog = smog

In urban areas, smoke and airborne pollution can attract water vapor (see p. 67) and cause fog to form. This mix of fog and pollution is called smog. In 1952, the Great Smog of London made 100,000 people ill and led to about 4,000 deaths—possibly many more. It was largely the result of burning coal. While coal is no longer used as a domestic fuel, today we get a different kind of smog from vehicle exhaust gases.

Yellow smog hangs over the modern city of Shanghai, China

Pockets of radiation fog fill the valleys at sunrise in the hills near Tainan, Taiwan.

1. Heat radiates from Earth's surface at night

3. Fog forms

2. Ground cools down, cooling lowest layer of air

Radiation fog

This type of fog is especially common in fall, when the air is still full of moisture from summer but temperatures can plummet at night. After sunset on a cold, clear, calm evening, the land radiates its heat into the atmosphere. As the ground cools, the lowest layer of air cools, too. When the air reaches its dew point, it becomes saturated: Water vapor is squeezed out and condenses into droplets. A fog forms that spreads slowly upward. Radiation fog usually "burns off" in the rays of the morning Sun.

If you **filled** an Olympic-sized swimming pool with **fog** and then **condensed** it, you would be left with **2 pints (1.25 liters)** of water.

Fog collection

In the Mexican desert, cacti have perfectly adapted to life in the intense heat of the desert. Small barbs on top of their conical spines direct droplets from fog down the spines to the stem where the moisture is channeled to the roots.

Fogs and San Francisco

San Francisco, California, is famous for its summer advection fogs. They start out at sea in a foggy "marine layer" of air as warm westerlies blow over the cool California Current. Hot air rising inland draws this foggy layer deep into San Francisco Bay, seen here shrouding Golden Gate Bridge. In winter, there are "tule" fogs instead which occur at night when surfaces cool quickly. Occasionally, tule and advection fog occur at the same time and mix together, creating a really dense fog.

URBAN WEATHER

STREET LIFE

A city is an island, not just of asphalt, brick, and concrete, but also of heat. Cities are hotter than rural areas: In the summer, for example, New York City is often 7°F (4°C) warmer than the surrounding countryside. Roads and buildings readily absorb solar energy by day, then give it off as heat at night. This "urban heat island" effect is most noticeable during heat waves. Air pollution is often a key factor of city weather, too.

Beating the heat

A spurting fire hydrant gives welcome relief from the heat for young New Yorkers in July 1961. Cooling off like this is a tradition. In 1925, the *New York Times* reported: "Small groups of children in bathing suits would gather about a hydrant. Then someone would get a wrench and open the hydrant and a stick would be placed in the nozzle to cause the water to spurt skyward and the children would jump under the shower."

Trapped air

Normally, air tends to get colder with altitude. But sometimes a temperature inversion occurs, in which cool air at the surface is trapped by a layer of warmer air above. When there is a temperature inversion over a city, the warm air layer acts like a lid that stops airbone pollution and smog (see p. 67) from dispersing upward, concentrating it near the ground, and causing a health risk. Low-lying cities or cities surounded by hills or mountains, such as Mexico City, can be particularly prone to temperature inversions.

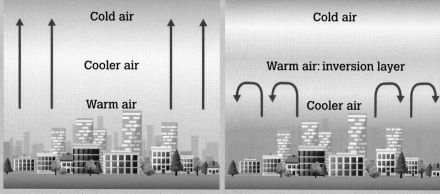

Normal conditions

Cold air
Cooler air
Warm air

Temperature inversion

Cold air
Warm air: inversion layer
Cooler air

Smog blanketing Mexico City

Temperature inversions can trap traffic fumes at street level.

Bengaluru, India, a city with dense traffic and high pollution

City pollution

The gases and particles released by burning fossil fuels in power stations, factories, homes, and vehicles creates severe air pollution in many big cities. The gases in vehicle exhaust fumes, for example, react in sunlight to form photochemical smog, which is largely ozone. Ozone in the stratosphere helps to shield us from harmful UV radiation, but at ground level it can cause serious breathing problems.

Heat map

Between buildings, it can seem shady. In fact, sunshine gets inside and is reflected back at the walls, warming the area even more. The contribution of buildings to urban heat can be seen in this thermal image showing Paris, France, early one morning during a heat wave. The hottest areas (red) are in the most built-up parts of the city. The coolest areas (blues) are mostly parks, woodland, and open spaces.

23°C
22°C
21°C
20°C
19°C
18°C
17°C

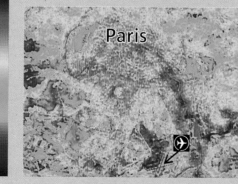

Paris

Paris surface temperatures at 8:18 am, June 28, 2019

Satellite image of Paris

Local weather

Many places have local winds so persistent that people give them names. In California, there is the scorching devil wind, the Santa Ana, which fans wildfires and is thought to drive people a little crazy! In the Mediterranean, there are the roasting, dusty sirocco and leveche that gust north from the Sahara. And in southern France, there is the famous mistral.

"Mistral" means "master" and they don't call it the master wind for nothing. It all starts in northeast France with the coming together of a low pressure zone to the east and a high pressure zone to the west. Together they squeeze a river of air between the Alps and the mountains of central France, and then a low to the south in the Gulf of Lion pulls it on with gathering force, until it reaches up to as much as 62 mph (100 km/h). It's no wonder that the traditional farmhouses of the area, called "mas," are all built facing southeast, with their backs to the mistral.

The mistral roars through with such ferocity that it can topple trains and hurl chairs across backyards. It gives boats a rough time but creates a paradise for windsurfers, who arrive from all over the world. Expect to see some amazing acrobatics! It can happen at any time, but the mistral blows hardest from December to April.

TRICKS OF THE LIGHT

SPECIAL EFFECTS

Like a magician, the sky plays visual tricks on us. Tiny particles split white light from the sun into its constituent colors and scatter them over the sky. This is why we get blue skies and red sunsets. Dust, water vapor, rain, and ice in the sky also create rainbows, mirages, and other special effects. Who knows, maybe you'll find a pot of gold at the end of the next rainbow that you see!

Spectacular sight
A rainbow arcs across the mountainous Tyrol region of Austria, just after a rainstorm. Its seven colors—red, orange, yellow, green, blue, indigo, and violet—are the colors in sunlight, refracted and reflected into concentric bands by the rain. There is always a second rainbow above the first, but it is usually too faint to see.

RAINBOW

BAND OF COLOR

A rainbow forms if the Sun is behind the viewer and low in the sky, and rain (or any another form of precipitation) is in front of the viewer. The sunlight is reflected inside a raindrop and changes direction (refracts) as it passes in and out of it. How much rainbow you see depends on the landscape and the angle of the Sun.

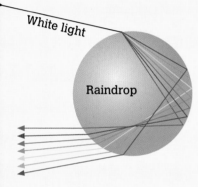

White light

Raindrop

Seeing a rainbow
What you see in a rainbow is the Sun reflected at varying angles from inside billions of raindrops. Rainbows are round because raindrops are spherical. Sunlight is made of every color, but raindrops bend each one differently. The color you see in each drop depends on how the Sun catches it. On the bow's outside, the Sun catches drops at a steep angle and you see red; on the bow's inside, the angle is shallow and you see violet.

Waterfall double rainbow
The colors in the fainter second rainbow are in reverse order because they have been reflected for a second time.

Upside-down rainbow
A circumzenithal arc (upside-down rainbow) occurs when sunlight refracts through horizontal ice crystals in cirrus clouds in the upper atmosphere.

Lunar halo
Each ice crystal in the high clouds acts as a miniature lens.

Sun halo
At the center is the Sun, with the circular halo around it. On either side are two bright spots called "sun dogs," or parhelia.

HALO

CIRCLE OF LIGHT

Halos around the Sun and Moon happen when a thin layer of cirrus clouds moves across the sky. The ice crystals in the clouds refract and reflect the light.

Mirage in the desert
What travelers see is a refracted image of the sky on the ground, which looks just like water.

MIRAGE

OPTICAL ILLUSION

Layers of air at different temperatures and density bend light. If the ground is hot and the air above it cool, light bends as it moves, creating a watery effect called a a mirage.

SPECTRE

GHOSTLY VISION

A really spooky effect, the Brocken spectre can happen if someone is positioned above the clouds, with the Sun behind them.

Eerie shadow
The viewer sees their own shadow because the light is reflected back at them from the clouds with a circular "glory" or halo around it.

Flying saucers?

Few sights in the sky have been mistaken for alien flying saucers more often than lenticular clouds. These amazing disc-shaped clouds form where moist winds blow over mountains. The way the air is forced sets up "standing" (non-moving) waves in the flow beyond. Lens-shaped clouds form in the crests of these waves.

WEIRD WEATHER

Flashing lights, clouds of frogs, and a scarlet Sun? Weather can get weird! Powerful winds can scoop up enough desert sand to color the sky, and heated air above the clouds may create enough energy for bursts of colorful lightning. Strange clouds whirl like alien spacecraft, and tornadoes and waterspouts can suck up frogs, fish, and other creatures before hurtling them back down as a very strange downpour!

A sand-and-dust haboob threatening Khartoum, Sudan

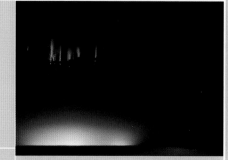
A group of red sprites soaring up above the top of a thundercloud

It's raining animals!
For nearly 200 years, in the Central American country of Honduras, the *Lluvia de peces,* or "rain of fish," has happened every year. In spring or early summer, a storm brings heavy rain and when it stops hundreds of fish are left flopping around on the ground. And no one is sure why! Throughout history there have been stories like this, involving fish, frogs, birds, worms—even snakes. It is most likely that they arrive via a tornado, waterspout, or are simply washed out of their homes by heavy rain.

Light displays
Large thunderstorms cause flashes of lightning in our skies, and also extraordinary light displays in the upper atmosphere called "transient luminous events" (TLEs). These include red sprites, vertical flashes above the cloudtops, up to 60 miles (95 km) high, and blue jets, which fan out up to 30 miles (50 km) above the clouds, before disappearing.

Haboobs
These extraordinarily powerful dust storms are created when powerful gusts of desert wind pick up sand, carry it along, and dump it. The name comes from the Arabic word *haab*, or wind, and these storms are common in the Sahara Desert, although if the conditions are right, they can occur in deserts worldwide. The downward wind of the haboob can reach wind speeds of more than 70 mph (112 km/h), and the storms can be 90 miles (145 km) wide.

A 1555 engraving recording a Nordic tale of raining fish.

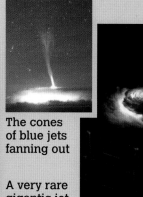

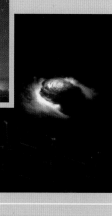

The cones of blue jets fanning out

A very rare gigantic jet

Hurricane Sun
In October 2017, a red Sun was seen high over England as the remnants of Hurricane Ophelia dragged in tropical air from north Africa. Desert sand and dust particles scattered all but the red wavelengths in the light from the Sun.

A colorful fire rainbow

A rare red Sun

Colored arcs in the skies
Fire rainbows, or circumhorizontal, arcs are an optical illusion created by the Sun and cirrus clouds. They can only occur when the Sun has risen higher than 58 degrees in the sky. At this angle, the light refracts through the ice crystals in the cirrus clouds, creating a rainbow. Moonbows, or lunar rainbows, are created by moonlight instead of sunlight and are even more rare.

A ghostly moonbow

In **2010**, it rained **live fish** on **Lajamanu**, a town in Australia, for **two days**.

DANGEROU

S WEATHER

BIRTH OF A HURRICANE

SPIRALING TROPICAL STORMS

Hurricanes are the most extreme weather the atmosphere can throw at us. These giant, circular storms roll in from the east across the ocean, and by the time they hit land they are so big you can only see them all from space. From above, they look like vast, whirling cream cakes. But their impact is anything but sweet. In just a few days, they can unleash the power of 10,000 nuclear bombs to assault places in their path with ferocious winds and torrential rain.

Hurricane season

The official hurricane season for the Atlantic Basin (the Atlantic Ocean, the Caribbean Sea, and the Gulf of Mexico) is from June 1 to November 30, with a peak from mid-August to late October. However, devastating hurricanes can occur anytime in the hurricane season.

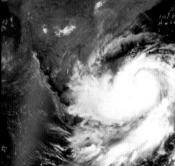

Tropical cyclone Fani heading toward India

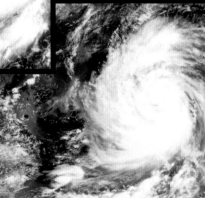

Typhoon Mangkhut hits the Phillippines

Hurricane by name

Hurricanes go by various names, but they're fearsome everywhere. They're called hurricanes in the Atlantic, typhoons in the north Pacific, and tropical cyclones in the Indian Ocean and the south Pacific. In the Atlantic, hurricanes are born in summer and fall off northwest Africa, near the Cape Verde Islands, and head westward to the

Category 5
In October 20 Michael made landfall in the Florida panhar

Hurricane Michael approaching the US coast

Intensity
Wind speed was about 160 mph (257.5 km/h) on landfall, gusting all the way to Georgia.

Getting disturbed

Hurricanes begin to stir into life in late summer as the tropical Sun beats down on the ocean and steams off water to build giant thunderclouds. High overhead, the cloud tops are skimmed by a jet of air streaming from the east. As it rushes out from the hot, dry Sahara over the warm seas, this jet develops meanders called "easterly waves," which round the stormclouds up into a mass called a "tropical disturbance."

Turning mass

If conditions are right, the disturbance begins to take shape. The easterly trade winds that blow here begin to curl round the disturbance, thanks to the spin of the Earth. Soon they gather the storms in and they all start turning as one mass—counterclockwise north of the equator and clockwise to the south. The updrafts are focused at the center and the pressure drops. The shapeless disturbance is now a spiraling tropical depression.

Moving on

Driven by the trade winds, the depression moves slowly westward, gaining power as it gathers in more clouds.

Tropical disturbance

Hurricane Florence

Tropical Storm Isaac

Hurricane Helene

Getting stormy

Before long, the depression has grown big and strong, not yet a hurricane but a tropical storm with strongish winds blowing round the center and rings of clouds full of rain. It doesn't move very fast, but it's moving night and day. In barely two weeks, it's driven across the ocean, and could develop into a full-blown hurricane.

The eye of a hurricane can measure **more than 200 miles (322 km) wide** and inside it the weather is **calm**.

Blowing a hurricane

From a satellite, a full-blown hurricane looks like a giant pinwheel. At the surface, torrential rain lashes down from rings of thunderstorms known as rainbands, while howling winds drive the storm. At the center of the storm is a clear "tunnel" through the clouds, called the "eye." Here, winds spiral up and out of the cloud walls. When the eye passes over, the sky clears and everything is calm. Don't be fooled—the lull is brief!

Suction effect
Low pressure in the eye raises the sea level below, causing a storm surge.

Spreading out
Cool, dry air flows outward from the center, sucking up more air from below.

Rainband
Thunderclouds are separated by zones of clearer air.

Wind direction

HURRICANE IMPACT

THE WORST WEATHER CAN THROW AT US

When a hurricane rolls in from the sea, dark, ominous clouds entirely fill the sky. The waves begin to churn and crash. And the winds begin to whistle, threateningly. Then, wallop! The hurricane comes in overhead, and as the cool lands sucks the energy from the storm, the clouds shed water in torrents. More than 12 in (30 cm) of rain can pour down in just a few hours. You're experiencing the most awesome, violent storm on planet Earth. But the worst may be yet to come . . .

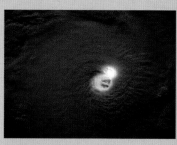

Quiet eye
After hours of battering, the rain stops. The winds ease off. Don't be fooled. This is the eye, the storm's quiet center, passing over. Within an hour, it's gone and the fury of the storm is back.

Strike 1
Soon after the rains start, the full fury of the hurricane lets rip, with winds of terrifying power hitting land. The noise is tremendous. Trees are bent over, and flimsy buildings are torn apart, and loose roofs flap wildly. In the strongest, Category 5 hurricane, the roaring wind is able to pick up cars and toss them over, and even wreak havoc with well-constructed buildings.

Danger
Storm surges and large waves are the greatest threats to life.

Strike 2
The waves whipped up by a hurricane can be frightening enough. But there's more. Low air pressure in the hurricane's eye can lift the ocean surface up in a dome called a "storm surge." As the hurricane moves landward, it drives the surge with it, creating a massive high tide that can swamp coastal areas and sweep far inland.

Storm surges flow tens of miles inland carrying coastal debris

Strike 3 and out!
Eventually, the storm moves on and away, the rains stop and the winds die down. But the storm has a nasty sting in its tail. The combination of torrential rain, massive waves, and the storm surge can dump a huge amount of water in low-lying coastal lands. Long after the storm passes, the waters can begin to rise. The flooding that follows many a hurricane is often its most devastating and long-lasting effect.

Hurricane force

To be classified as a hurricane, a storm must have winds of at least 74 mph (118 km/h). These are known as "hurricane force" winds, but in a mighty hurricane, winds can get much stronger. In Hurricane Irma in 2017, winds gusted to 185 mph (298 km/h)! As hurricanes approach, storm watchers in the US try to give each storm an intensity rating on the Saffir-Simpson scale to warn people what to expect.

TROPICAL CYCLONES 1945–2006

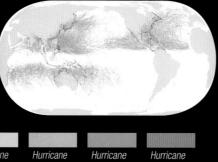

| Tropical depression | Tropical storm | Hurricane Category 1 | Hurricane Category 2 | Hurricane Category 3 | Hurricane Category 4 | Hurricane Category 5 |

THE SAFFIR-SIMPSON SCALE

Category One
74–95 mph (119–153 km/h), storm surge 4–5 ft (1.2–1.5 m) low-level damage: mobile homes shifted, signs blown over, branches broken.

Category Two
96–110 mph (154–177 km/h), storm surge 6–8 ft (1.8–2.4 m) moderate damage: mobile homes turned over, roofs lifted.

Category Three
111–130 mph (178–209 km/h), storm surg 9–12 ft (2.7–3.6 m) extensive damage: Small buildings wreck trees uprooted.

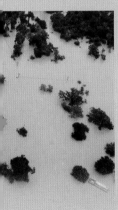

Aerial view of flooding caused by Hurricane Harvey, 2017

Eye change
After the eye passes over, the wind blows from your left as you face the ocean.

4

5

Category Four
131–155 mph (210–249 km/h), storm surge 13–18 ft (4–5.5 m) extreme damage: most trees blown down, widespread structural damage to all buildings, large scale flooding.

Category Five
over 155 mph (over 250 km/h), storm surge over 18 ft (5.5 m) catastrophic damage: most buildings destroyed, forests decimated, roads and pipelines wrecked; devastating flooding.

KATRINA
TIMELINE OF A HURRICANE

In 2005, Hurricane Katrina devastated the Gulf Coast of the United States, and particularly the Louisiana city of New Orleans. The 350-mile-wide (563-km-wide) storm started over the Atlantic Ocean, made landfall in Florida, then spun into the Gulf of Mexico. There, warm waters powered up a whirling ring of storms with 175 mph (280 km/h) winds that whipped up giant waves and broke through New Orleans's protective floodwalls and levees, nearly destroying the city.

Left behind
The Superdome (above) sports stadium and the Morial Convention Center were used as the main "shelters of last resort" for stranded New Orleans residents. Neither building escaped damage from Katrina but they were the safest places around for the thousands of citizens left behind whose homes had been destroyed or flooded.

Hard-hitting disaster
Katrina was a Category 5 hurricane (see pp.88–89) and the most devastating storm ever to strike the United States. The city of New Orleans was hit especially hard because 50 of the levees built to prevent its waterways flooding failed. Water poured in and the residents who had not evacuated found themselves surrounded by up to 20 ft (6 m) of water.

Formed (as a tropical depression): August 23, 2005

Dissipated: August 31, 2005

Category: Category 5 hurricane

Main areas affected: Florida, Louisiana, Mississippi, Alabama

Highest sustained winds: 175 mph (280 km/h)

No. of dead: 1,833

Damage: more than 1 milllion displaced, more than 80 percent of New Orleans flooded

Cost: $108 billion

Landfall
Now a hurricane measuring 25 miles (40 km) across, Katrina makes landfall at 7p.m. between North Miami and Hallandale beaches on Florida's southeast coast.

Gaining in strength
The National Hurricane Center warns that Katrina is becoming stronger as it travels across the very warm waters of the Gulf of Mexico. The governors of Louisiana and Mississippi declared a state of emergency.

Supplies
The Louisiana National Guard prepare three truckloads of water and seven truckloads of ready meals to deliver to the Superdome. The supplies are enough for 15,000 people fo three days. However, 25,000 people arrive at the Superdo and are there for five days.

Katrina's progress
The first that most people knew of a potential hurricane was a weather warning issued by the National Hurricane Center on August 23. It warned that a tropical depression was forming over the Bahamas. No one could have guessed the

Wednesday, August 24
Katrina is named and is about 230 miles (370 km) east of Miami, Florida, with winds blowing at 40 mph (65 km/h).

Thursday, August 25
Katrina makes landfall in southeast Florida as a Category 1 hurricane with 80 mph (130 km/h) winds.

Friday, August 26
Katrina briefly weakens before it passes over the Gulf of Mexico and strengthens to a Category 2 with 105 mph (170 km/h) winds.

Saturday, August 27
Katrina becomes a Category 3 with 115 r (185 km/h) winds .President George W. B declares a federal state of emergency for Louisiana. Hurricane hunter aircraft int the hurricane to collect data.

The levees break

On August 29, what many people had feared happened—the levees cracked and broke under the pressure of a massive storm surge. Water poured over and through the levees and, one by one, districts of the city were inundated. Of the 284 miles (457 km) of levees and floodwalls, approximately 169 miles (272 km) were damaged.

"Thank God I left when I did because a few seconds after I got upstairs [Katrina] ripped off the entire side of the house." Elizabeth Ashe Havrilla, eyewitness

Evacuation
The National Weather Service describes Katrina as "potentially catastrophic," and the mayor of New Orleans, Ray Nagin, issues a mandatory evacuation order. Tens of thousands begin to stream out of the city, jamming the roads with vehicles of all kinds.

Rescue
The storm passes, but stranded people have to be rescued from attics and rooftops. They are taken to high ground to be evacuated.

Katrina dissipating over Ohio

Aftermath
Katrina ruined homes and lives all along the Gulf Coast, and left whole communities under water. Tens of thousands of volunteers from all over the United States provided help with food, shelter, clothes, and health care.

Sunday, August 28
Everyone in New Orleans is told to evacuate and the Superdome opens as a shelter for those who cannot leave. Katrina becomes a Category 5 hurricane with wind speeds of 175mph (280 km/h).

Monday, August 29
Katrina makes its second and third landfalls as a strong Category 3. A 27-ft (8-m) high storm surge smashes into the levees protecting New Orleans, which begin to fail, and water pours over them into the city.

Tuesday, August 30
Katrina moves away from New Orleans and weakens into a tropical storm. But about 60,000 people are still trapped in the city, some on their roofs, many in the Superdome and the Morial Convention Center.

Wednesday, August 31
Water stops flowing into New Orleans, but most of the city is flooded. Katrina dissipates over Ohio. A public health emergency is declared in Louisiana, Mississippi, Alabama, and Florida.

After the storm

A military truck drives down a flooded Canal Street, New Orleans' historic thoroughfare, on August 31, 2005, the day after Hurricane Katrina moved away from the city. More than 400,000 residents had evacuated, many never to return, with damage to property costing tens of billions of dollars.

A New Orleans-based contractor Joe Bridges and his family were among the last residents to leave the city. They initially planned to ride out the storm, but decided to evacuate at the last minute.

"When the levees broke," Joe said, "everybody was in complete shock as to what we are gonna do next?"

"It felt like packing was just, like, a quick rush," Joe's son, Jordan, said. "You know, grab the pictures, grab our important documents, grab a few days of clothes. As I'm seeing people wade across Canal Street in bins, I'm like, 'We're probably not going home.'"

The Bridges family returned to New Orleans in January of 2006.

"I just remember [it] being an emotional few days," Jordan said.

One outcome of the the disaster was a desire by many people to get more actively involved in their communities. During and after the storm, individuals and communities had pulled together to help each other out.

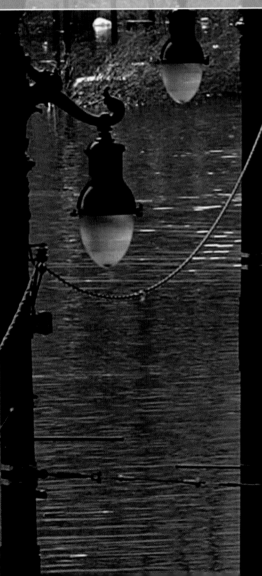

Helicopter evacuation

Extreme weather can take only minutes to cause carnage and leave residents trapped and fearing for their lives. On August 30, 2017, a Category 4 hurricane named Harvey swept through Beaumont, Texas, causing catastrophic flooding. Here, a CBP Air and Marine Operations aircrew lifts stranded residents to safety.

TO THE RESCUE

When extreme weather puts people in danger, real-life heroes risk their own safety to rescue them. Some rescuers are professional lifesavers, while others are trained volunteers who give up their time for free and often have regular "day" jobs. Animals, such as dogs, are part of the rescue team, too.

First response
Extreme weather conditions can make it very difficult to reach those affected, but drones can help. They can be sent ahead of the rescue team and speed up the rescue effort by locating people. Drones can also deliver first-aid kits and other emergency supplies.

Drone with medical kit

Airplane dropping water on a forest fire in Italy

Fighting wildfires
During wildfire season, firefighters risk their own safety to bring rapidly spreading blazes under control. Planes and helicopters can also be used to support firefighters on the ground, dropping thousands of gallons of water, often mixed with chemical retardants, to try and douse the fires from the air.

The most **successful** mountain rescue **dog**, was a **St. Bernard** named **Barry** that worked in the **Swiss Alps** in the early **1800s**—he **saved** more than **40 people**.

Sea rescue
The night of September 7, 1838, in Northumberland, England, brought a terrible storm. Lighthouse keeper's daughter, Grace Darling, and her father, rowed out from their lighthouse (right) in a small boat to save the survivors of a wrecked steamship. This heroic story has inspired generations of heroes at sea. In the US, the Coast Guard is responsible for safety at sea, while in other countries it's often down to volunteers.

UK lifeboat on a rescue mission

Rescue boats in Thailand, 2011, when 8.2 million people were affected by flooding

Working together
When monsoons or hurricanes turn streets into waterways, organizations such as the police, coast guard agencies, and the army join forces, along with intrepid volunteers to search for and rescue stranded residents.

Search and rescue (SAR) dogs
For people trapped under flood or storm-damaged buildings, specially trained dogs are often their best hope. The canine heroes are trained to detect a human scent—when they find it, they either lead their handler to the spot, or stay and bark an alert.

Medic and rescue dog search a collapsed building in the Ukraine

Mountain rescue team with slide stretcher

Mountain rescue
These teams battle some of the most extreme conditions, such as blizzards, and the most dangerous terrain, from glaciers to crevasses. Often it's not safe to deploy a helicopter, so the mountain rescue team have to combat freezing weather, to rescue injured people from perilously high altitudes.

Storm starters

All year, a slab of chilly air sits over the Arctic Ocean, oozing south to create the polar front where it comes up against warm, moist air driven by westerly winds. It's here that the low pressure zones or depressions at the heart of frontal storms begin. In fall especially, groups of lows are blown eastward by the westerlies. As each moves, kinks in the front develop into two arms—a cold front and a warm front—that bring a distinct sequence of stormy weather as they pass over.

Air masses collide

The polar front develops where cold polar and warm tropical air masses collide. Cold air flows east on one side and warm air flows west on the other.

Cold air mass
Warm air mass

The cyclone begins

The polar front develops a small bulge, as warm air slides up over the cold air, creating the beginnings of a low pressure zone or depression.

Cold air mass
Warm air mass

Two fronts develop

The bulge sharpens into a V-shaped kink, with two fronts —a warm front on the leading edge, and a cold front on the trailing edge. This brings stormy weather as the fronts pass over.

Cold air mass
Low
Warm air mass

Fronts closing

The cold front moves faster than the warm front, and begins to catch it up. The storm begins to lose some of its power and the depression weakens.

Cold air mass
Low
Warm air mass

Occluded front

Eventually, the cold front entirely catches up with the warm front, merging with it and lifting it right off the ground to form a single front called an occlusion.

Cold air mass
Low
Warm air mass

FRONTAL STORMS

EVERY-DAY STORM DRAMA

If you see feathery wisps of cirrus overhead in the west, beware! The sky may be blue now, but there's a high chance that a brutal frontal storm will roll over you in just a few hours. Frontal storms, or extratropical cyclones, flare up along one of the atmosphere's great battle zones, the polar front. They might not be as dramatic as cyclones in the tropics (hurricanes). But they can bring very, very rough weather— and are much colder!

In full force

Here in Binalong Bay, Tasmania, Australia, the dramatic skies show that a frontal storm is on its way. Pretty soon the waves will build, and those on the coast should be prepared for a short, but spectacular storm. Chilly frontal storms are common in this part of the world during the winter months.

Wild west?

Whoosh!! Frontal storms can whip up mountainous waves as they are blown eastward across the ocean. The wave tops turn white with salty spray. And when they hit land, these storm waves smash against west coasts with tremendous force. They are best viewed from a safe distance away.

The storm rolls over

As a frontal storms rolls in from the west, it brings a familiar sequence of stormy weather as first the warm front then the cold front pass over.

Warm front

1. The first sign is cirrus clouds high up in the west at the leading edge of the warm front. Get ready for rain in 6–12 hours. The breeze is easterly.
2. As the warm front comes on, the sky is flecked with cirrostratus, and the Sun may have a halo. Air pressure drops and a southeasterly wind stirs.
3. Soon, altostratus and then nimbostratus clouds darken the sky. It starts to drizzle, then rains for hours, until the base of the warm front passes.
4. When the rain stops, the skies clear, leaving cumulus and stratocumulus. The air is warmer, but it's just a lull before the cold front hits …

Cold front

5. As cold air muscles in along the cold front, it shoves up the warm air sharply, piling up vast and stormy thunderclouds. Pressure rises.
6. The winds veer sharply southwest, and the clouds burst, bringing torrents of rain. The sky may flash with lightning and roar with thunder!
7. Fortunately, the cold front is steeper and passes in an hour or so. The rain stops and the wind drops to leave clear, cold air and a few fluffy cumulus clouds scudding through the sky.

Pyrocumulonimbus

This type of cumulonimbus is formed by fires, such as wildfires (see pp. 184–185). Its storms can spread the fire farther, while lightning can spark more fires.

THUNDERHEAD

HOW STORMBRINGERS WORK

Cumulonimbus clouds mean trouble! Also known as "thunderheads," these vast, threatening giants bring rain and thunderstorms. Towering high into the sky, they can inflict extreme weather—torrential downpours, lightning, and hail, and they can also be breeding grounds for tornadoes. Their impact is often short-lived, except when grouped into long-lasting multicell or supercell storms.

How cumulonimbus forms

A cumulonimbus begins life below 6,500 ft (2,000 m) as a fluffy white cumulus cloud (see pp. 58–59). As warm, moist air moves upward from Earth's surface, the cumulus grows taller and becomes a cumulonimbus. The dense moisture in the cloud becomes rain, and the falling rain pulls cool, dry air down with it, creating a downdraft, and potentially a storm. Storms require a lot of energy, so they are usually short-lived. When the downdrafts become stronger than the updrafts, the storm weakens and dissipates.

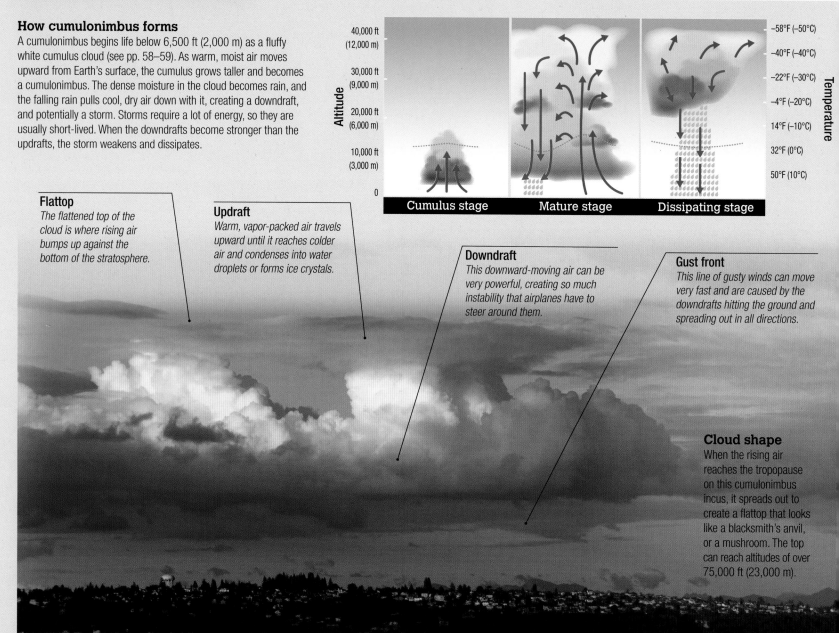

Altitude	Temperature
40,000 ft (12,000 m)	−58°F (−50°C)
30,000 ft (9,000 m)	−40°F (−40°C)
	−22°F (−30°C)
20,000 ft (6,000 m)	−4°F (−20°C)
	14°F (−10°C)
10,000 ft (3,000 m)	32°F (0°C)
0	50°F (10°C)

Cumulus stage   **Mature stage**   **Dissipating stage**

Flattop
The flattened top of the cloud is where rising air bumps up against the bottom of the stratosphere.

Updraft
Warm, vapor-packed air travels upward until it reaches colder air and condenses into water droplets or forms ice crystals.

Downdraft
This downward-moving air can be very powerful, creating so much instability that airplanes have to steer around them.

Gust front
This line of gusty winds can move very fast and are caused by the downdrafts hitting the ground and spreading out in all directions.

Cloud shape
When the rising air reaches the tropopause on this cumulonimbus incus, it spreads out to create a flattop that looks like a blacksmith's anvil, or a mushroom. The top can reach altitudes of over 75,000 ft (23,000 m).

Thunderhead lightning

Violent air currents in thunderheads smash hail, ice and water droplets together, charging them with static electricity. Positive charges build up at the cloudtop, negative ones at the base, and the ground also gets positively charged. The difference in charges becomes so great that lightning—a flash of electricity—leaps to equalize the difference (see pp. 100–101). Lightning creates thunder, but since sound travels more slowly than light, you do not hear it until some time after the lightning flash, depending on how far away the cloud is.

Types of cumulonimbus

Cumulonimbus, like most other clouds, has different types. The forms of this impressive giant can be identified by their distinctive appearances.

Cumulonimbus calvus—cloud below the tropopause that has not formed an anvil.

Cumulonimbus capillatus—the stage between calvus and incus, with a hairlike top.

Cumulonimbus virga—wispy rain from cumulonimbus that evaporates on the way down.

Cumulonimbus praecipitatio—forerunner of a thunderstorm, it gives heavy, short-lived rain.

LIGHTNING STRIKE

ENERGY BLAST

A single bolt of lightning can shoot a billion volts of electricity through the air. The flash we see is an electric charge zapping within a cloud or between the cloud and the ground, and the energy it blasts out sends a shockwave through the air that we hear as thunder. Lone trees and all buildings make prominent targets for lightning strikes—the Empire State Building in New York was once struck eight times in 24 minutes!

Air around a **lightning bolt** is **superheated** to 54,000°F (30,000°C)—more than **five times hotter** than the surface of the **Sun!**

Lightning strike
Most lightning flashes inside the cloud, linking top and bottom. But some goes to ground, beginning with negative charges zigzagging down. This is the "stepped leader." When it's close to the ground, a positively charged "streamer" zooms up to meet it. With the path now complete, a huge negative flow zaps to the ground while the brilliant flash we see races back upward.

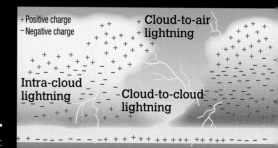

How lightning starts
As ice and water droplets collide, some lose electrons, making them positively charged, while others gain them, becoming negatively charged. Positive particles gather at the top of the cloud; negative particles gather at the base. Once the difference gets extreme, lighting flashes between them.

Most lightning happens inside clouds, which produce about ten times as many flashes as cloud-to-ground lightning.

Cloud-to-ground lightning

Cloud-to-cloud lightning

Lightning flashes inside a thundercloud

Ball lightning—an unusual and rare event

World records

The most lightning strikes in the world happen above the Catatumbo River in northwest Venezuela, at a rate of 1.2 million per year. And Roy Cleveland Sullivan (1912–1983), US park ranger in Shenandoah National Park, Virginia, holds the record for being hit by lightning and surviving—seven times in 35 years.

Most lightning strikes happen where the Catatumbo River empties into Lake Maracaibo

US park ranger Roy Cleveland Sullivan. His wife was also struck by lightning when hanging out her laundry!

Around the world

Around the world there are around four million lightning strikes every day. This map shows the lightning strike frequency from 1995 to 2002. The information was collected by satellites and shows places where there were less than one flash a day on average (gray or light purple) through to the deep red of places that were struck frequently. The equator is warmer than the poles, so thunderstorms and lightning are widespread in the tropics.

St. John's weather bomb

On the night of January 17, 2020, the town of St. John's in Newfoundland, Canada, was pounded by a truly incredible snowstorm. Over 30 inches (76.2 cm) of snow fell that night, and winds roared through the town, at times gusting over 90 miles per hour (145 km/h). This was a blizzard of truly epic proportions.

Because of the ferocious wind, the snow was piled up into giant snowdrifts. One side of a house might be buried up to the attic while the other side was almost snow free. As the blizzard howled on, people stayed indoors, and the next morning many woke up to find just a wall of snow greeting them as they opened their front doors.

St. John's had been hit by a weather bomb. These are the hurricanes of the midlatitudes. But while hurricanes typically take many days to develop, bomb cyclones develop so quickly that meteorologists call it "explosive cyclogenesis" or "bombogenesis."

Bomb cyclones are, fortunately, rare events. Typically, just one per year hits the east coast of North America, in early spring or late fall, after developing out at sea. They form after a warm air mass slams into a cold air mass, forcing the warm air to rise so suddenly that at a latitude of 60°N, pressure can drop 24 millibars in just 24 hours.

SUPERCELL

BIRTHPLACE OF TORNADOES

Supercells are the bucking broncos of the skies—huge masses of air churning around and bouncing off each other to create spinning whirlpools. Formed from thunderhead clouds (see pp. 98–99), these storms can freeze supercooled waterdrops into giant hailstones, and generate the strongest winds on Earth at speeds of up to 250 mph (400 km/h).

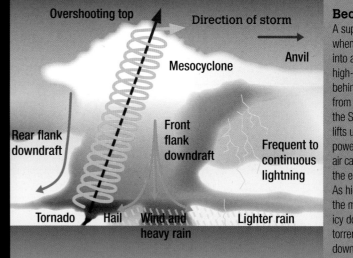

Overshooting top

Direction of storm

Mesocyclone

Anvil

Rear flank downdraft

Front flank downdraft

Frequent to continuous lightning

Tornado Hail Wind and heavy rain Lighter rain

Becoming super

A supercell gets nasty when its "tail" is twisted into a rolling tube by high-level winds from behind and surface winds from the front. Warmed by the Sun, this rolling tube lifts upright to become a powerful vortex of rising air called a mesocyclone—the engine for a tornado. As high-level winds tilt the mesocyclone forward, icy downdrafts and torrents of rain tear down in front.

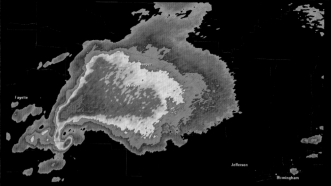

Radar imaging

Meteorologists are able to recognize certain features in radar images of supercells and give the public advance warning of approaching storms. In this image, the hook shape at the bottom left indicates that tornadoes are forming in a supercell approaching Birmingham, Alabama on April 27, 2011.

Microbursts and macrobursts

Intense downdrafts called microbursts and macrobursts turn into damaging winds on the ground. Microbursts are smaller but produce stronger winds up to 170 mph (270 km/h). There are two types of microburst, wet and dry. Wet microbursts produce intense rainfall at ground level, but in dry microbursts precipitation often evaporates before it reaches the ground. Macrobursts are more than 2.5 miles (4 km) wide and with winds up to 135 mph (215 km/h).

A wet microburst produces a curtain of rain

Grassland giant

Supercells form when there is enough wind shear and instability in the atmosphere. They are most common in the central part of the United States, but may occur in other parts of the world. This enormous rotating supercell with its curtain of rain has formed above the vast pampas grasslands of Argentina. These fearsome storms occur at any time of the day, but mostly in the late afternoon, when the ground and air have been heated by the Sun, causing warm air to rise and clash with sinking cold air.

Warning signs

A tornado develops quickly, but there are often clues that one is coming. The first warning, though, is often via the TV or radio. When there's a tornado warning, you have to move, fast.

Greenish sky

Dark, low-lying cloud

Large hail

Loud roar
(like a freight train!)

TORNADOES
DANGEROUS TWISTERS

Swirling out from huge supercell storm clouds, tornadoes can unleash some of the fastest, deadliest winds on Earth. Most tornadoes are short-lived, developing quickly and lasting only 10–15 minutes, but they can leave behind a trail of devastation. The safest place to shelter from a tornado is underground.

Cold air mass   Vortex

Warm mass

Tornado touchdown!

This image is created from multiple photos of a single tornado as it formed from a supercell north of Minneola, Kansas, on May 24, 2016. The storm went on to produce at least 12 tornadoes, and at times there were two or three of these on the ground at the same time. Five of the tornadoes were EF3, and three EF2.

Enhanced Fujita scale

This scale rates the strength of tornadoes based on the damage they do when they pass over vegetation and structures erected by people. Only a small percentage are destructive, the vast majority of tornadoes do little damage.

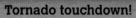

EF0
Light damage
Breaks branches off trees; damages chimneys and signboards

EF1
Moderate damage
Rips surface off roofs; moving vehicles blown off roads; mobile homes overturned

EF2
Considerable damage
Flips over cars; tears off some roofs; large trees snapped or uprooted

EF3
Severe damage
Derails trains; roofs and walls torn off houses; many trees uprooted; cars lifted off ground

EF4
Devastating damage
Houses leveled; cars and large objects hurled over a distance

Tornado formation

When warm, moist air soaring upward in a supercell is blocked by higher, cooler winds, it is sometimes whipped into a whirling funnel of air, or vortex, that tilts. Cool downdrafts then push the vortex back toward the ground, and as soon as it touches the land, it becomes a tornado.

Destructive
Homes, power lines, trees, and vehicles were damaged.

EF5
Incredible damage
Missiles hurled through the air over a greater distance; most things in its path destroyed

Most devastating

An EF5 tornado can do enormous damage. On June 22, 2007, this tornado struck the town of Elie in the Canadian province of Manitoba. It was 330 yd (300 m) wide as it traveled through Elie, destroying houses and the town's mill. The damage it caused cost $46.7 million in today's money. Since 1950, 59 tornadoes have been rated EF5 in the US.

The Wonderful Wizard of Oz

In L. Frank Baum's 1900 children's novel, a tornado picks up a Kansas farmhouse with a young girl, Dorothy, and her pet dog, Toto, inside and deposits it in the magical Land of Oz. In 1939, the movie based on the book was the first time an authentic-looking tornado had been seen on-screen.

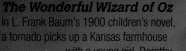

Waterspouts

While tornadoes form over land, rotating cloud-filled waterspouts occur over water. Waterspouts are usually much weaker than tornadoes, although a few are equally as dangerous, with high winds, large hail, and frequent lightning strikes. Some move from water onto land, where they become tornadoes, but they dissipate quickly. In turn, tornadoes sometimes move out to sea and become waterspouts. The Florida Keys see more waterspouts than anywhere else—up to 500 of them a year.

Scene of devastation

In Tornado Alley (see pp. 110–111), tornadoes are such a frequent occurence that people retreat into specially built storm shelters if a tornado approaches. Here, young girls emerge from a storm shelter in Moore, Oklahoma, to find their home completely destroyed after an EF5 tornado tore through the town's suburb.

Lucky escape
The storm in May 2013 killed 24 people, injured more than 200, and left thousands without homes.

Tri-state tornado

On March 18, 1925, the deadliest tornado in US history moved from southeastern Missouri through southern Illinois to southwestern Indiana. Its 219-mile (352-km) journey, the longest recorded, was up to 1 mile (1.6 km) wide and lasted for more than three and a half hours.

It left 695 dead, 2,027 injured, 15,000 homes destroyed,and $1.6 billion of damage in today's money. Here, the northwest corner of West Frankfort, Illinois, lies destroyed.

West Frankfort was a mining town. When the electricity went out, the miners went to the surface to meet a scene of utter devastation. Of those killed in their town, most were women and children.

Francis Redshaw was seven years old at the time. He later recalled that the shock of the tornado left people in a daze. Feeling that something awful had happened they did not know how to respond. When some of the injured began to cry for help, a spell was broken and hundreds of men, women, and even children rushed to the devastated part of the city. Before darkness fell, 150 dead were counted, and the injured had filled the miner's hospital plus several temporary hospitals set up in churches.

TORNADO ALLEY

DEADLY PATH

The United States is blasted by about 1,000 tornadoes a year, more than any other country. About half travel along "Tornado Alley," which runs through the Great Plains, a 3,000-mile (4,800-km) area of flat land between two mountain ranges, the Rockies and the Appalachians. The tornado season is typically in late spring.

Tornado touchdowns
These are the main states that form Tornado Alley. However, over the last four decades, there have been signs that Tornado Alley is shifting toward the east to include large area of the Midwest and many southeastern state

1884

EARLY RECORD

This is said to be the oldest known photograph of a tornado. It was taken on August 28, 1884, around 22 miles (35 km) west of Howard, South Dakota. It was one of four strong tornadoes in the area that day.

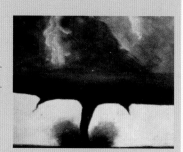

Tricky subject
The picture was taken by F. N. Robinson, a Howard resident. The tornado demolished a farmhouse, killing four people and injuring two others. It is possible that the photograph has been doctored.

1925

DEADLIEST TORNADO

The 1925 Tri-State tornado (see p. 108) was probably an F5, although the Fujita scale was not introduced until 1971. It moved over 219 miles (352 km) across Missouri, Illinois, and Indiana, at speeds of 70 mph (113 km/h).

FIRST PICTURES OF STORM DISASTE
HERALD EXAMINER
1,000 DEAD, 3,000 HURT LATEST TOL OF TORNAD
In the Twinkling of an Eye, Murphysboro Was No More

No warning
The tornado took everyone by surprise. The word "tornado" had been banned from weather forecasts since the late 19th century to prevent panic, the forecast for March 18 was normal, and radar was not yet invented.

2018

TWIN TORNADOES

Twin twisters are a rare phenomenon and occur when a storm produces two tornadoes that spin independently of each other and at different EF speeds. The weaker of the two twisters is described as a "satellite" tornado.

Two at once
On May 28, two tornadoes touched down simultaneously on the plains of eastern Colorado, causing crop damage. These two tornadoes stemmed from the same supercell but are visibly different from one another.

2019

FOUR-STATE TORNADO OUTBREAK

In just a single day, March 3, 2019, at least 40 tornadoes touched down in four states in the southeastern United States—Alabama, Georgia, Florida, and South Carolina. This is farther south and east than the area that has until recently been called Tornado Alley.

Be warned
This is a map of the tornado warnings issued to the public on March 3 by the National Weather Service. They used data and tornado reports sent to the Storm Prediction Center from across the four states. When tornado watches are issued they warn people to be prepared. Tornado warnings say "Take Action!"

LEGEND
SPC Tornado Reports (Filtered)
Tornado Warnings
(12 UTC March 3 - 12 UTC March 4)

1:30 p.m.	5:17 p.m.	5:34 p.m.	5:41 p.m.	5:42 p.m.	5:45 p.m.	5:46 p.m.	5:50 p.m.	5:58 p.m.	6:12 p.m.
The National Weather Service issues a TORNADO WATCH	The National Weather Service moves to a TORNADO WARNING	It touches down 0.5 miles (0.8 km) southwest of Joplin city limits	The tornado moves across 32nd street and south Black Cat Road	Now an EF4, it travels across Maiden Lane and hits the Medical Center	The tornado passes Main Street and strikes Joplin High School	It strengthens to EF5, and hits major retailers along Range Line Road	Continuing to destroy homes, it begins to weaken and dissipate	Now an EF3, it flips cars and sweeps away some interstate signs	The tornado weakens and dissipates completely southeast of Joplin

2011

TIMELINE OF A MULTI-VORTEX TORNADO

In one of the deadliest and costliest years for tornadoes in the United States, a massive multi-vortex tornado hit the town of Joplin, Missouri, on May 22. It left behind it a scene of devastation. Only a few supercells spawn multiple tornadoes at the same time, and a multi-vortex tornado is one that has at least two smaller tornadoes swirling around the main vortex.

Peak winds: EF5, over 200 mph (320 km/h)

Path length: 22.1 miles (35.5 km)

Dead: 161

Injured: over 1,150

Homes and businesses destroyed: over 7,000

Cost: $2.8 billion (in today's money)

Before and after the tornado
Comparative images of Joplin show the damage that a tornado can inflict. Such information is vital for rebuilding and helping to prepare for future tornadoes.

Catastrophic destruction
The tornado left behind an unrecognizable landscape of shattered structures and torn and twisted metal. At its height, it destroyed hundreds of houses, leveled a nursing home and a school, and left only a concrete vault where a bank had stood.

On the alert
Storm chasers look out for radar images of a debris ball, an area of high reflectivity at the end of the storm's hook.

STORM CHASERS
GETTING UP CLOSE

Most sensible people stay clear of tornadoes, but some folk run toward them. Storm chasers like to experience the raw power of nature up close. They monitor forecasts to try and predict where a twister might hit, then head straight for the front line to gather firsthand data and amazing footage of these powerful, dangerous storms.

Radar dish
This gathers atmospheric data and sends it to the onboard computer.

Chasing the storm
Professional storm chasers will drive thousands of miles to get near some of the most dangerous tornadoes on Earth. With wind speeds of 300 mph (480 km/h) and a habit of changing direction suddenly, the storm chasers need to understand when it is okay to get close and when it is best to retreat. Over the years, storm chasers have been able to provide scientists with invaluable data about how tornadoes behave, so they can more accurately predict what future tornadoes might do.

Car rooftop weather station
Australian storm chaser Clyve Herbert adjusts his mobile weather station as a severe storm builds.

Preparing for the storm

Chase vehicle
These research vehicles have three computers onboard, two in the back and one in the front.

Cup anemometer
The stronger the wind blows, the faster the three plastic cups turn.

Essential equipment
A digital camera, a laptop, GPS, and mobile internet feeds, two-way radios, and food are minimum requirements for a storm chaser. An anemometer (left) is also essential as it is used to measure wind speed and direction. Some vehicles carry other instruments, to be deployed when the tornado hits.

Pod deployment
Special pods are designed for tornado low-level wind and damage studies, to collect data on temperature, humidity, wind speed, and air pressure.

Stand
This stand holds the DOW steady in windy conditions.

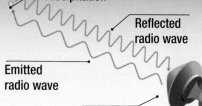

Precipitation

Reflected radio wave

Emitted radio wave

Transmitter

Imaging the storm
Doppler radars can be driven into position as the storm develops to scan the atmosphere at low levels and establish how much precipitation there is and what other particles are present. Radio waves are beamed from the Doppler and strike objects in the atmosphere. This scatters their energy, with some of it reflected directly back to the radar. Modern Dopplers can transmit energy pulses both horizontally and vertically to give a 3D image.

Chasing vehicles

From state-of-the art government vehicles to amateur creations, every storm chaser needs a a set of wheels that's tough, and fast.

Tornado Intercept Vehicle (TIV 2), from which the inside of a tornado was filmed

DOW 7, part of the Dominator series owned by the Center for Severe Weather Research

The National Severe Storms Laboratory (NSSL) mobile command truck in 2010

NSSL's Mobile Mesonet Probe vehicle with custom-designed rack, 2017

Doppler on Wheels

Packed with technology, Dopplers on Wheels (DOWs) have to be fast enough to keep pace with twisters and tough enough to withstand their force. The radar dish is the key part of the vehicle and it must be light enough to be carried on the back of the truck, but big enough to pack serious radar capabilities. DOW radar made the first 3D maps of tornado winds and the first maps of multiple vortex structures in tornadoes.

Rotating arm
The radar rotates 360° to gather maximum data.

Flashing lights
Extra lights make the DOW more visible in stormy weather.

Control center
Inside is a compact control room with computer and radio equipment.

RAPID X-POL

BLIZZARD

WHITEOUT!

There's probably no harsher weather than a blizzard. Bitter cold and high winds combine to create a ferocious snowstorm. Visibility vanishes in a mass of white, and icy blasts rip across the landscape, hurling the snow into drifts. Movement becomes almost impossible, and the intense cold from both the snow and the wind chill can be lethal for anyone caught in the open.

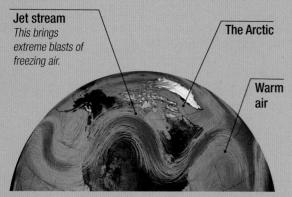

Jet stream
This brings extreme blasts of freezing air.

The Arctic

Warm air

Blizzard conditions

In North America and Siberia, you can get a blizzard when the polar jet stream wanders south in winter, letting cold air direct from the Arctic roll in. The trouble begins when it clashes with warm, moist air from the south. The cold air forces the warm air up, creating great, chilly clouds. When these clouds let their load fall, it hits icy-cold Arctic air beneath and stays frozen as snow.

What is a blizzard?

In the US, 150 years ago, a "blizzard" meant a volley of rifle shots. But in the 1870s, a newspaper in Iowa used the word to describe a snowstorm. The term stuck. Now meteorologists define a blizzard as a snowstorm with winds of at least 35 mph (56 km/h) that lasts for at least three hours and cuts visibility to 0.25 miles (400 m) or less.

Driving in blizzard conditions is extremely dangerous.

Watch out for blizzard warnings

Whiteout

When a power outage makes all the lights go out, it's called a blackout, so when a severe blizzard hits, it's called a whiteout. The term also has a more specific definition in polar regions—it's when the snow coverage is so thick that nothing casts a shadow, the horizon isn't visible, and only dark objects are discernible.

Blizzard winds

Snow combined with piercing winds makes blizzards terrifying. They blow snow into snowdrifts and hurl balls of ice at anyone trying to walk in the storm. The air is cold enough anyway but the wind can create a powerful wind chill, making it feel 70°F (20°C) colder. The wind chill is the way air feels much colder when the wind is blowing.

Ground blizzard

It doesn't have to be snowing to be a blizzard. Ground blizzards occur when a fierce wind lifts and drives snow and ice already on the ground. One of the most tragic blizzards of all was the Children's Blizzard of 1888, which killed about 235 people on the Great Plains. Although there was snow on the ground, there had been a mild spell immediately before, so when the blizzard struck many were caught out in the open in light clothing.

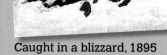

Caught in a blizzard, 1895

Snow corridor

The "roof of Japan," the Tateyama Kurobe Alpine Route passes through Mt. Tateyama in the Japanese Alps. Snow walls are carved each spring in this area, which experiences some of the heaviest snowfalls on the planet. The walls can reach more than 65 ft (20 m) high!

"Storm of the Century"

The blizzard that hit the east coast of the US on March 12, 1993 (see map to right), was one of the worst in US history. The "Superstorm of '93" not only brought a very wide 1–3 ft (0.3–0.9 m) dump of snow. It was also blasted along by Category 5 hurricane force winds, piling up snow in drifts as high as a house. Roads and airports were shut for days, and it caused up to $11 billion in damages, killing more than 300 people.

(inches)
0
4
10
20
30
+50

Dust storms

There may not be much rain in desert regions, but there is plenty of dust! And sometimes vast choking clouds of it can be hurled up into the air by roaring thunderstorms, or by vicious winds whipping along a weather front where cold air undercuts hot, dry air. As the dust cloud whirls up into the air, the wind drives it forward in a terrifying wall—the world goes dark and you need to take cover.

The most famous dust storms are the "haboobs" of southern Sudan (see p. 83). Indeed, they're so famous that dust storms are often called haboobs all around the world. The Sahara Desert, which supplies the dust for haboobs, is the world's biggest source of windblown dust, and fine Saharan dust can ride the winds up into Europe, or even across the Atlantic, bringing yellow air and vivid sunsets. It can even make people in Miami feel like they're choking.

Camels are fantastically well-adapted to haboobs. They have a third, clear eyelid that protects their eyes from blowing sand, and two rows of long lashes that help do the same. Sand up the nose isn't a problem for these desert creatures. They can shut their nostrils right up!

Landslides

On February 17, 2006, a massive debris avalanche destroyed an entire village in Southern Leyte, Philippines. Three days later, marines search through the rubble for survivors. More than 1,000 people died and several million pesos worth of crops, livestock, and fisheries were damaged by flooding. The landslide was triggered by 10 days of heavy rains and a minor earthquake.

MOST DEVASTATING

We may understand the weather better today, but we can hardly control it. Meteorologists can warn people that hurricanes, floods, snowstorms and droughts are on their way, but they can still have a devastating impact. Dangerous weather can bring deadly conditions for anything in its path, and humans can't always get out of the way. Here are some of the most devastating weather events ever.

Hankou City Hall floods, 1931

Mississippi River flood, 1927

Hurricanes
Although hurricane warning systems are improving all the time, it's not always possible to predict the size or path of a hurricane. In October 2018, Hurricane Michael hit the Florida Panhandle. It was actually a Category 5 when it reached the coast, with winds estimated at 160 mph (260 km/h). It left 16 people dead in Florida alone.

Drifts in New Jersey, March 1888

Snow
Blizzards bring some of the harshest weather on the planet (see pp.114–115). The Great Blizzard of 1888 paralyzed the east coasts of North America and Canada. The 45 mph (72 km/h) winds drove snow into drifts of up to 50 ft (15 m) high. People could not go anywhere for a week—there were 400 deaths, 200 were in New York City alone.

Hurricane Michael is one of only five Category 5 hurricanes ever to hit the US.

Flooding
The destruction caused by flooding can be catastrophic. In 1927, the Great Mississippi Flood displaced more than 630,000 people living near the river. In 1931, a series of devastating floods hit parts of China, causing the deaths of up to 4 million people. After a three-year drought, meltwater and heavy spring rain combined to create the disaster.

70% of worldwide wildfires in an average August are in **Africa.**

Wildfires
In December 2019, 150 wildfires raged across east Australia, fanned by high wind gusts of up to 50 mph (80 km/h). (See pp. 184–185.) Australia was not the only country to suffer— during that year, massive wildfires tore through vast areas of forest from Brazil to Africa, and from California to Indonesia.

Stranded cattle after a bushfire, Namibia

Patterns of drought in Rainbow Valley, Northern Territory, Australia

Drought
Drought (see p. 188) affects more people globally than any other natural disaster. In every month of 2017, extreme drought affected at least three percent of the land on Earth. Prolonged drought causes economic hardship, and increases wildfires and the spread of diseases.

WEATHER

WATCHING

Goddess of the sky

In ancient Egypt, Nut was celebrated as goddess of the sky. It was said that she swallowed the Sun god Ra at night and gave birth to him every morning—an interesting explanation for the pattern of day and night. Here, she is depicted on an object found in the tomb of the pharaoh Tutankhamun, her blue skin representing life and rebirth, while her wings are spread to protect the dead.

MYTHS AND LEGENDS

Before science and technology, humans had to find other explanations for the causes of our weather. In Australia, icicles were thought to be hurled by sisters who had fled Earth; in Japan, it was the Snow Woman who made storms to send people to sleep; while in Africa, rainbows were giant snakes.

Groundhog Day

Every year on February 2, thousands of people gather to see a groundhog named Phil emerge from his burrow in Punxsutawney, Pennsylvania. Legend has it that if the groundhog sees his shadow on Groundhog Day, there will be six more weeks of winter. Inspired by German traditions, it was started in 1887 by local newspaper editor Clymer Freas.

Groundhog (*Marmota monax*)

Phil's **predictions** have been **correct** about **39 percent** of the time.

Italian house tile depicting Aeolus controlling the winds

Sun god

In many cultures, the weather could only be explained by a divine being. In Hinduism, Surya is both the Sun and the Sun god. In early Hindu scriptures, known as the *Vedas*, which date back to 1500 BCE, he is depicted as the source of energy and light. He rides in a chariot drawn by seven horses.

Surya, Hindu god of the Sun

God of thunder

In Norse mythology, Thor was the god of thunder and protector of humankind. He was portrayed as a powerful being with a huge hammer called Mjölnir. When Thor struck Mjölnir on the ground, humans heard the sound as thunder.

Thor surrounded by depictions of Mjölnir

God of the winds

The ancient Greek god Aeolus was said to have been appointed by Zeus, the king of the gods, to be the guardian of the winds. Aeolus could control the winds and release them whenever he wanted, usually at the command of Zeus or any other god who wanted to cause a great storm.

The Rain Queen

To the Balobedu people of Mpumalanga, South Africa, the Rain Queen is a vital part of their culture and history, and the only female traditional ruler in the coutnry. Called Modjadji, the queen rules over more than 100 villages and is said to be a living incarnation of the rain goddess. It is believed she has mystical rainmaking powers and is able to send storms to destroy her people's enemies or gentle rain to help their allies.

Annual rainmaking ceremony

Hurricane god

The Aztecs believed that Tezcatlipoca was one of the four gods who created the world. He was the god of the night sky, with special powers over the hurricanes. Legend has it that he fought with his brother Quetzalcoatl, the god of wind. Tezcatlipoca is often shown with one foot as legend also has it that he lost the other when the world was created.

TOMORROW'S WEATHER

CRUNCHING IT OUT

Not so long ago, if you wanted to know tomorrow's weather, you couldn't do much more than look at the sky and guess. Nowadays, weather forecasting is a huge global effort. Countless machines monitor the atmosphere nonstop. Giant supercomputers are crunching data. And hundreds of thousands of meteorologists are forecasting.

Number crunching

To generate a forecast, meteorologists take millions of measurements from across the globe at set times, at a grid of locations and heights in the atmosphere, including temperature, humidity, wind, and air pressure. Powerful computers crunch these numbers to calculate general future values, and forecast the weather ahead.

Weather forecast model; 5-10 minute measurements

Changes between columns and levels are calculated

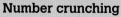

Variables at the surface:
Temperature
Humidity
Pressure
Moisture Flux
Radiation Flux

Variables in the atmosphere:
Wind vectors, humidity, clouds, temperature, height, precipitation, aerosols

Weather models

Numbers alone mean very little. To make the numbers work, weather forecas[ters] have models—theories about how different aspects of the atmosphere work, as seen below. They might, for instance, have a model for how a cloud develops. They set up the computer with this model. When the computer is fed new data, it will follow this model to give a forecast.

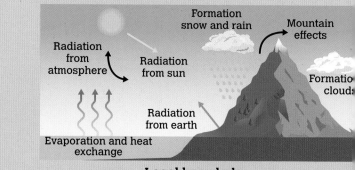

Formation snow and rain

Mountain effects

Radiation from atmosphere

Radiation from sun

Formatio[n] cloud[s]

Radiation from earth

Evaporation and heat exchange

Local knowledge

Supercomputers aren't always so good at picking up local features, which can have a big impact on the weather, such as a nearby hill or lake. So experienced weather forecasters make their own observations of local conditions to make more precise local forecasts. That doesn't just mean looking at the sky; it also means looking at radar and satellite images, and taking measurements of atmospheric conditions.

The butterfly effect

In 1972, meteorologist Edward Lorenz asked, "Does the flap of a butterfly's wings in Brazil set off a tornado in Texas?" to illustrate how a tiny event can trigger major storms, through a series of knock-on effects. This is called "chaos theory," and it's a big problem for forecasters, which they try to solve with ensemble forecasting (see p.139).

Forecasts then and now

In the 1850s, people began to use the newly invented electric telegraph to give people advance warning a frontal storm was on its way. Then, British naval officer Admiral Robert FitzRoy (1805–1865) realized that the telegraph could send into his office simultaneous observations of weather conditions from widely spread locations. With this method, he saw that weather patterns are repeated, and so he could make forecasts of how they might develop. He made the first newspaper weather forecasts.

Flutterby

Lorenz didn't mean that the butterfly's flutter actually causes a tornado— just that there are so many variables that little changes or fluctuations can make a massive difference.

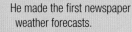

Daily newspaper forecast

Digital forecast

How do you get your weather forecasts?

WEATHER WATCHERS

24/7 GLOBAL EFFORT

Around the world, every minute of the day, instruments and meteorologists are recording and observing conditions in every corner of the atmosphere. It's a gigantic, nonstop, global effort. Not a single change can happen without it being flagged. Nearly a quarter of a billion weather observations are recorded every single day, and sent to supercomputers around the world for processing.

What are they measuring?
The key observations are temperature, humidity, precipitation, air pressure, wind speed, and wind direction. Most measurements today are electronic, though some people still use traditional instruments, like this water gauge.

AUTOMATIC RECORDING

COLLECTING DATA

Sometimes there's someone on hand to take the reading, but meteorologists need measurements from remote areas, from far out at sea, and from every level in the atmosphere.

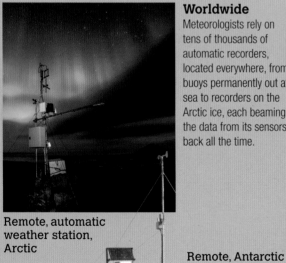

Worldwide
Meteorologists rely on tens of thousands of automatic recorders, located everywhere, from buoys permanently out at sea to recorders on the Arctic ice, each beaming the data from its sensors back all the time.

Remote, automatic weather station, Arctic

Remote, Antarctic weather station

Brilliant buoys
Moored buoys can provide hourly data about wave heights and frequency. Hurricane buoys are now used in the Atlantic, very strong, with a good backup system in case of a powerful storm.

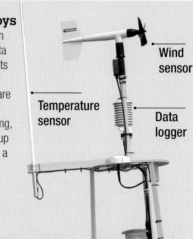

Wind sensor

Temperature sensor

Data logger

Large, moored buoys are used near shore

Drifting buoys are used far out at sea

Chesapeake Bay Interpretive Buoy System
877-BUOYBAY
www.buoybay.org

OCEAN BUOYS

SEA FORECASTERS

Bobbing out at sea around the world are hundreds of floating buoys equipped with instruments to sense the weather. Some are moored in the same place by long anchors to the sea floor. Others are allowed to drift with the ocean currents. The Tropical Ocean Array is 70 buoys moored in deep water along the equator in the Pacific, which is crucial in monitoring El Niño events.

SUNSHINE HOURS

BEFORE DIGITAL

In the old days, devices were much simpler! Hours of sunlight were recorded by a Campbell-Stokes recorder. This had a glass ball that focused the Sun's rays to burn a paper strip.

The Campbell–Stokes recorder
As the Sun moves through the sky, the burn mark moves. If clouds block the Sun, the burning stops. Nowadays, sunshine hours are recorded on electronic devices.

DUST-SPOTTING

ATMOSPHERIC DUST

Laser beam
Laser pulses are sent into the atmosphere and scattered by aerosols. The scattered light is detected by telescopes.

Aerosols are particles in the atmosphere that provide the "seed" for water droplets to condense. Without them, clouds don't form. They also reflect and absorb solar radiation. Laser beams, such as this one at the Leibniz Institute for Tropospheric Research (TROPOS) in Germany, can measure aerosols at altitudes of up to 9 miles (15 km).

All kinds of aerosols
TROPOS examines all kinds of aerosols, from mineral dust, sea spray, volcanoes, and human-made, from industry and traffic. We know that aerosols have a big effect on global climates. This project should help us find out more.

WEATHER BALLOON

HIGH-ALTITUDE INFORMER

Every day, twice a day at the same time, a thousand hydrogen-filled balloons are released into the atmosphere from all over the world. These balloons are called "radiosondes" because of the instruments they carry that beam data back to Earth. They fly up, slowly, through the air, automatically recording weather data.

Balloons are filled with hydrogen or helium

High flier
After about two hours, they reach about 18.6 miles (30 km) up and the balloon bursts. The instrument packs parachute back to Earth for recovery, but many are lost.

Balloons can be used to determine flight conditions

Weather balloon in western Australia

Measuring ice in the Arctic

The Arctic is the world's refrigerator. It gives off more heat to space than it absorbs, which helps cool our planet. But a dramatic change is taking place in Arctic weather. Over the past 30 years, the Arctic has warmed more than any other region on Earth. Sea ice and snow cover is disappearing, and glaciers are retreating.

In September 2019, an icebreaker ship set sail from Norway to the Arctic Ocean, in the largest polar expedition ever. It will stay close the the North Pole for a year, through a polar winter. The data it gathers will be used by scientists around the globe to study the Arctic's climate in the most detailed way ever.

About 60 scientists and technicians are aboard for two months at a time, taking detailed measurements of the ice and snow, ocean, atmosphere, and the organisms of the central Arctic.

Markus Rex, the expedition leader, described what it's like being in the middle of a frozen ocean in a 24-hour polar night:

"It's very striking. All the colors disappear—just the white snow and the ice and the black of everything behind, on this completely frozen landscape. There's a feeling of being on some different planet or moon."

WEATHER STATIONS
GLOBAL NETWORK

We couldn't get the forecasts we do without the vast global network of weather stations, monitoring the weather night and day. The World Meteorological Organization (WMO) collects data from 10,000 ground-based stations, as well as 1,000 high-altitude stations, 7,000 ships, 100 moored and 1,000 drifting buoys, hundreds of weather radars, and 3,000 aircraft. Stations are evenly spaced and carefully located away from buildings, trees, and hills which might distort readings. Weather stations collect a mixture of snapshot hourly observations of the weather and daily summaries from all around the world.

Local station
This "cooperative" weather station, part of the Weather Bureau network, was set up in Granger, Utah, in the 1930s. The first weather observers were volunteers, but in 1938 the bureau hired five official observers and a full-time forecaster.

Handheld station
Today, weather stations can be be small enough to fit in your hand, and operate in extreme conditions. This digital weather station is monitoring the meltwater on the Greenland ice sheet. Miniature sensors report the data, shown on the screen.

Wind vane
This registers which direction the wind is blowing from.

Anemometer
Wind-driven cups are attached to a generator that spins around to measure wind speed.

Standard equipment
Automatic Weather Stations (AWSs) transmit or record observations. Most are made up of the these instruments (left and below) and the measurements they take are converted into electrical signals and then transmitted by wire or radio. Some weather stations simply store data until it is collected.

Radiation shield
Temperature and humidity probes are housed in this radiation shield that also protects from rain and snow.

Visibility sensor
The system includes a transmitter, receiver, and processor that record visibility by measuring by what degree light is scattered.

Rain collector
The rain gauge provides daily, monthly, and annual rainfall tracking.

Data logger
This collects the data and transmits it by wire or radio, or archives it until it is collected.

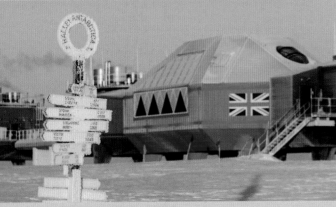

Mobile weather station
Built on a floating ice shelf in the Weddell Sea, Antarctica, the Halley VI Research Station is made up of modules that sit on skis. It is part of the WMO's Global Atmosphere Watch program, providing reliable information on the chemical composition of the atmosphere.

Low cloud envelops the Tai Mo Shan Weather Radar Station

Protective dome
This dome protects the radar dish, somewhat ironically, from the weather.

Radar weather station

The Tai Mo Shan Weather Radar Station sits on top of the highest peak in Hong Kong. Its large radar dish is housed inside a dome that protects it from the elements. It uses Doppler radar to measure the distance to rain, snow, or hail by emitting pulses of microwaves. Precipitation scatters the microwaves, sending some energy back to the transmitter, and the intensity of this signal, or radar echo, provides data on the distance and wind speed of any approaching storms.

Satellite dishes
These receive information from other weather networks around the world.

Transmitter
This tower sends out weather reports from Tai Mo Shan.

Extreme locations

Some weather monitoring takes place in the most remote places on Earth, a challenge to place and a challenge to maintain.

Remote rainfall gauge in the northern Tien Shan mountains of Kazakhstan

Desert peak solar-powered weather station near Las Vegas, Nevada

Arctic automated weather station under the northern lights, Spitsbergen, Norway

Rocky island off the coast of Thailand in the Andaman Sea of the Indian Ocean

WATCHERS IN SPACE

BEST VIEW IN THE UNIVERSE

Satellites in space give weather watchers an amazing grandstand view of the atmosphere. In a single image, they can show an entire hurricane, then track it minute by minute as it develops. Indeed, satellite images can show anything from variations of temperature across a single town to the global circulation of winds. Using satellites is called "remote sensing" because it collects data from a distance, and it's come to be as important as what we can see from Earth.

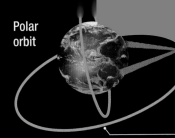

Polar orbit

Geostationary orbit

Which way around

"Polar-orbiting" satellites loop nonstop north–south around the poles about 530 miles (850 km) up, taking picture after picture as they go. The picture path runs not north–south as you might expect, but in an S, running westward—because the Earth is spinning all the time. "Geostationary" satellites don't move at all, relative to the Earth. Instead they sit 22,370 miles (36,000 km) up, going around with the Earth as it spins so they stay above exactly the same place all the time.

Watching the weather

Since 1975, the Geostationary Operational Environmental Satellites (GOES) operated by NASA and NOAA, have provided scientists with continuous atmospheric data and imagery as well as information on solar activity. GOES-16 can provide a composite image of Earth every 15 minutes and targets areas with extreme events like hurricanes, wildfires, or volcanic eruptions every 30 seconds.

Space Environment In-Situ Suite (SEISS)
Contains sensors to monitor fluxes in the magnetosphere

Space weather detection sensors
Monitors solar energy and particle output that can damage satellites and electrical grids on Earth

Advanced Baseline Imager (ABI)
An imaging radiometer that visualizes clouds, rainfall, snow cover, and other atmospheric conditions on Earth

X-ray sensors
Observe the Sun to warn of solar flares

Extreme Ultraviolet and X-ray Irradiance Sensor (EXIS)

Solar Ultraviolet Imager (SUVI)
A telescope monitors complex active regions of the Sun

Geostationary Lightning Mapper
(GLM) Maps frequency, location, and extent of lightning to predict extreme weather

Active and Passive

Some satellites just take pictures of the atmosphere below. Satellites like these are called "passive." Others are "active." That means they send out beams of microwaves. When the beams hit tiny things in the air such as raindrops, hailstones, snowflakes, ice pellets, and even birds, they are scattered. Some are bounced back right to the satellite's antenna and detected.

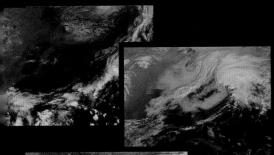

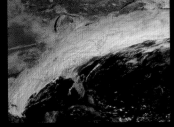

"Passive " photos from GOES satellite of the US west coast

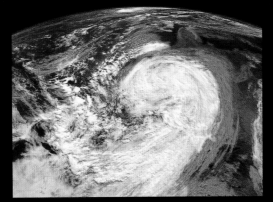

Visible

Some satellites take pictures of the cloudtops using visible light, like photos down on the ground. Basically, they show how brightly the sunlight reflects in different places. They can reveal the thickness of clouds—the thicker the cloud, the more brightly it reflects sunshine. They can show the difference between snow and clouds from other landscape features. But they can't tell you about rain, and they don't work on Earth's night side!

Doppler radar

Doppler radar is remote sensing from the ground, not satellites. Just as airport radar detects planes in the air, so weather radar detects things by bouncing microwaves off them. With a special kind of radar called Doppler radar, hurricane watchers, for instance, can build up a detailed map of where and how much rain is falling. It can even give an indication of the wind speed.

Solar array,
Has five panels of photovoltaic cells generating more than 4,000 watts of power from sunlight

Sun sensors
Used to detect and adjust angle to the Sun and control altitude

Maps detect heat energy from land and water

Thermal infrared
Like night vision cameras on the ground, infrared satellites detect the pattern of heat either on the cloudtops or on the ground. They show cold spots and warm spots very clearly. They can even tell you how high the cloudtops are—the colder the cloudtop, the higher it must be.

Water vapor monitor
Water vapor monitors use infrared, like thermal imagers. But they are specially tuned to detect radiation from water vapor in the upper atmosphere. They can detect it not just in clouds but in clear skies. So they help show how the air is moving everywhere, not just cloudy areas.

Factory producing carbon dioxide as a waste product.

Climate change watch
In 2018, Japan launched a special satellite called IBUKI-2. "Ibuki" is Japanese for breath, and the IBUKI-2's task is to monitor greenhouse gases in the atmosphere, especially carbon dioxide and methane. These are the gases that cause our climate to warm. The satellite is beginning to not only show changing levels of these gases In the air—but exactly where they are originating.

HOME WEATHER

BECOME A WEATHER WATCHER

How's the weather where you are? If you're interested in weather, become a weather watcher yourself! You only need a backyard or balcony to set up your own weather station, or you can simply look out of a window. It's all about observations and making records of what you see. With a bit of practice, you can even start to make your own forecasts. Professionals can give you the big picture, but only you can track the weather going on right around you!

Sky photos

Photos are a great way to record the weather. You can take pictures and videos to see how the sky changes day to day, and also make a record of big events like thunderstorms or unusual cloud patterns.

Weather diary

Keeping your own weather diary is simple. Every day at the same time, maybe in the morning and evening, make a note of the outdoor temperature, the wind strength and direction, and the kind of clouds you can see in the sky. This is what meteorology is all about—keeping detailed, systematic records so you can learn to identify patterns. Some days, you could take readings at intervals during the day.

Cloud cover

You can also use photos to record the cloud cover every day. Using landscape format, take a picture of exactly the same place in the sky each day. Look at your photo and divide it into eight equal rectangles—either on a screen or on a print-out. Then work out whether each is more cloudy or more clear. Add up clear versus cloudy to get an "okta" reading.

Keeping records of the weather is what **meteorology** is all about

"Okta" cloud cover grids

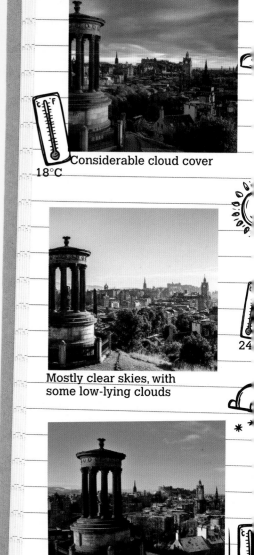

Considerable cloud cover
18°C

Mostly clear skies, with some low-lying clouds

Clear skies with some wispy clouds
24°

Weather journal

Here's an example of how you might track the weather in your local area.

Digital weather station

If you've got a little money, you can get yourself a complete digital weather station for about $70. They're amazingly comprehensive. They automatically record temperature, humidity, wind speed and direction, air pressure, and much more. You can plug the console into your laptop to keep a record.

Making a weather box

You can make your own weather box. You'll need a sturdy plastic or wooden box that can stand on its side. Paint it white. Using adhesive putty, stick your thermometers to the inside. Then find a sheltered spot outside and stand it so the thermometer is upright.

Weather hero

Thinking of becoming a meteorologist? Check out June Bacon-Bercey. She is widely considered to be the first African American female meteorologist and the first female TV meteorologist in the US. Her interest in science began in high school.

Cloud cover

Use these symbols to record cloud coverage in your weather journal.

Symbol	Cloud cover
○	0%
◐	10%
◔	20–30%
◑	40%
◑	50%
◕	60%
◕	70–80%
◑	90%
●	100%

Weather symbols

You can use official weather symbols for your journal or you can make them up! American Edward Augustus Holyoke did this as far back as 1742 in the Boston area!

Computer capacity
This high-performance supercomputer, "Mistral," is used in Germany to investigate model-based simulations of global climate change and its regional effects.

After devastating hurricanes like Sandy and Harvey, **supercomputer forecasts** have the power to **save lives.**

DIGITAL GENIUS

COMPUTER POWER

When you see a weather watcher crouched on a hilltop in a rainstorm taking readings, weather forecasting doesn't look like a high-tech business. But if you go behind closed doors at the major weather centers, you'll find some of the biggest, most powerful computers ever built. Ensemble forecasting (see p. 138) has improved the accuracy of forecasting a lot in recent years. It couldn't be done without supercomputers.

Early computer
The IBM 7090 computer was used for forecasting in the early 1960s. Its processing power was about 0.00001 percent of the processing power of your desktop computer!

SUPERCOMPUTER

The National Oceanic and Atmospheric Administration (NOAA) in the United States is in the process of creating a pair of linked Cray computers. When finished, in 2022, each will have the computing power to run at 12 petaflops—that's 12 quadrillion little calculations or floating-point operations per second (FLOPS). By comparison, a really good laptop can do 100 gigaflops (100 billion flops), that's a million times slower!

The more observations weather supercomputers can use, the more precise their forecasts are likely to be. The biggest can handle over 200 billion weather observations every day. But it's not just about recording the data.

PREDICTING DISASTER

The supercomputers then feed the numbers into theoretical models of the atmosphere. When they run these models, they predict all the figures for the future, too, and present it all onscreen in graphs, maps, and pictures that the weather forecasters can understand. What's more, supercomputing power allows forecasters in many locations to access and manipulate the data on their own screens.

When dangerous weather situations develop, such as the approach of a bomb cyclone or tornado, time is critical. The supercomputer can save time by sending out emergency warnings to authorities and even the public, though spoken alerts can sound alarmingly robotic!

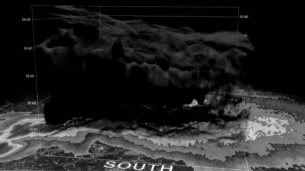

3D radar tornado model

Radar has long been used to detect rain. But since the 1980s, radar can "see" which way it's moving and how fast it's going, which is like being able to actually see the wind. The ability to see the winds inside of a thunderstorm is a huge deal. Meteorologists can warn of tornadoes in much better time, saving countless lives. This image shows the multiple-vortex Tuscaloosa–Birmingham tornado in Alabama in 2011.

Ensemble forecasting

Weather forecasting with computers relies on data taken by weather stations around the world. These numbers give the computer an accurate picture of the current state of the atmosphere. Then the computer's model uses these numbers to make a forecast.

In theory. The problem is, the atmosphere is pretty chaotic. So tiny, undetectable variations in the original data can be massively amplified. Famously, meteorologist Edward Lorenz said the atmosphere was so chaotic that a butterfly fluttering its wings could set off a tornado some weeks later, through knock-on effects. So just a minute flaw in the original data can make a computer forecast wildly inaccurate.

Meteorologists get around this problem by ensemble forecasting. The idea is to run the forecast model on the computer multiple times, as represented on these globes, each with slightly different starting conditions. The complete set of forecasts is known as the ensemble. The ensemble gives a range of possible forecasts. While weather forecasters may occasionally turn out to be badly wrong with a single forecast, they can be confident that the weather will usually be within the range predicted by the ensemble.

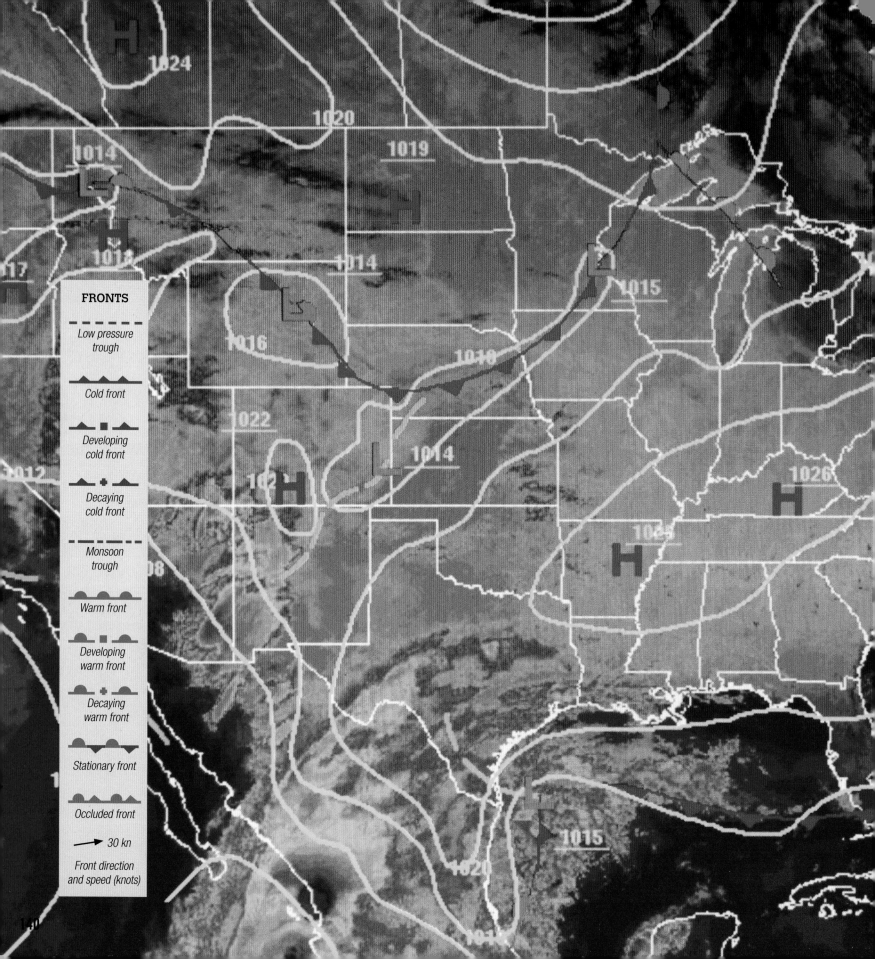

FRONTS

- - - - - - - Low pressure trough

▲▲▲ Cold front

▲▪▲ Developing cold front

▲✚▲ Decaying cold front

- ▪ - ▪ - Monsoon trough

⌒⌒ Warm front

⌒▪⌒ Developing warm front

⌒✚⌒ Decaying warm front

⌒▽⌒▽ Stationary front

⌒⌒ Occluded front

→ 30 kn

Front direction and speed (knots)

WEATHER MAPPING

CHARTS OF THE ATMOPSHERE

For centuries, weather maps were the only way to give a clear picture of the weather over a wide area. They let you see the weather pattern instantly, for example, and see what weather was on the way, and how bad. These charts give an overview of conditions at a particular time. Look out for the places where fronts are meeting; it's time for some turbulent weather!

The most obvious features on the map are isobars—long, curved lines joining points of equal pressure, usually in millibars. In some places they loop around to form complete circles. In the center there is an "H" or "L" to indicate a high pressure center, where the air is sinking, or a low pressure center, which is usually the focus of a storm. If isobars are close together, it indicates a sharp pressure drop and strong winds.

Colored lines with spikes or half discs show fronts. A blue line with spikes is a cold front; a red line with half discs is a warm front. The spikes and half discs point the way it is moving. Some charts have arrows indicating wind direction and strength, too. The most detailed show temperatures, cloud cover, humidity, visibility, and rainfall or snowfall, each with its own symbol. TV weather and media forecasters still sometimes use maps like these to help show the weather. Computer technology, with exciting graphic displays and clever animations has opened up new ways of presenting the weather, but weather maps are still a familiar sight.

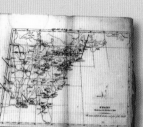

Early maps
This map is from 1953 but the first weather map was made in 1816 and it was drawn by hand. In the US, in the 19th century, a network of observers reported back to the Smithsonian to help create maps.

American sunshine
Map shows good weather spreading: Close isobars, low pressure (1004 mb), and rain clouds (orange) show a storm clearing away east (right), leaving the highs (H) of fine weather in the southwest (lower center), and the spikey blue line of a mild cold front crossing the Midwest (top left).

"The US Army Signal Corps was responsible for weather maps in the late 19th century."

Symbol	Weather
◗	Drizzle
≡	Fog
△	Hail
∞	Haze
●	Rain
▽	Shower
⧖	Sleet
⌐⌐	Smoke
✳	Snow
⏚	Thunderstorm
↯	Hurricane

Symbol	Wind speed (mph)
⊸	1–4
⊸	5–8
⊸	9–14
⊸	15–20
⊸	21–25
⊸	26–31
⊸	32–37
⊸	38–43
⊸	44–49
⊸	50–54
⊸	55–60
⊸	61–66
⊸	67–71
⊸	72–77

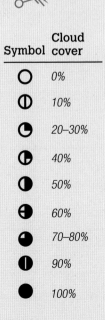

Symbol	Cloud cover
○	0%
◐	10%
◔	20–30%
◑	40%
◐	50%
◕	60%
●	70–80%
◕	90%
●	100%

TRUE OR FALSE?

YOU BETTER BELIEVE IT!

Long before the advent of scientific weather forecasting, people used to look for clues in the natural world to predict what weather to expect. Sailors and farrmers who were out in the open all the time and noticed little signs that a change in the weather was coming. Some old weather beliefs were just superstition, but some were based on close observation. Here is just a tiny selection of people's wisdom.

Halo, rain

"When halo rings the Moon or Sun, rain's approaching on the run" goes one saying, and it's true. Halos appear when the Moon or Sun shine through high-level, cirrostratus clouds. These clouds usually precede a warm front, so halos are a good sign that rain is indeed coming soon—except in cold winter weather, when the halos are an indicator of icy air.

"Red sky at night, shepherd's delight . . ."

This weather warning is so ancient it even appears in the Bible. But scientists can't quite pin it down. Sky colors certainly change with atmospheric conditions. And in many regions, weather comes from the west where the Sun sets, so the sky does show weather to come. But some scientists think the red is the Sun filtering through dry, dusty air, indicating dry weather to come. Others say the red is caused by storm clouds, meaning it will rain in the night but be clear by morning.

Biblical
"Red sky at night" first appears in the Book of Matthew in the Bible's New Testament.

All at sea
This warning is traditionally for sailors, not shepherds, in many places.

". . . Red sky in the morning, shepherd's warning"

The Sun rises in the east, so weather systems driven by westerly winds are traveling toward it. Red skies in the morning may be the low Sun catching the undersides of high clouds that precede a storm front, so they could indeed be a sign of rough weather to come.

Chewing the cud
Some scientists do believe that cows moo in certain ways to tell other cows about the weather!

Forecasting by cows

Animals can certainly sense changes in the atmosphere that we humans can't. But it's really hard to figure out just how. People used to believe that cows lying down was a sign of rain to come. But it seems cows simply lie down when they want a rest. People also thought that a cow with its tail to the east warned of bad weather, and there maybe some truth in this one. Cows like to have their backs to the wind, so this may indicate an east wind, which brings more unsettled weather.

Groundhog Day

According to folklore in North America, you can tell a lot from the weather on Groundhog Day on February 2, the day a groundhog traditionally comes out after its winter sleep. If the weather is cloudy, then spring will come early. If it is sunny, the groundhog will see its shadow and retreat back inside, and it will be chilly for another six weeks. So they say . . .

Kelp is found in forests under the sea

Kelp warning

Kelp seaweed is a surprisingly healthy food, and in the past many people would collect it from the seashore and hang it out to dry, ready for cooking later. Many believe hanging kelp is a good weather indicator, responding to changes in air humidity. If the weather is fine, the seaweed dries out and shrivels. If rain is on its way, it will swell and go limp and damp.

Ash

Oak

"If the oak comes out before the ash . . ."

An old saying was that "If the oak comes out before the ash, we shall have a splash; if the ash comes out before the oak, we shall have a soak." The idea was that if the oak buds first in spring, the coming weeks will bring just light showers, but if the ash buds first then there will be downpours. Scientists have found no evidence that this is true in any way!

WEATHER FORECASTS

PREDICTING THE WEATHER

Most of the time we need weather forecasts to help plan our everyday lives—whether we need to carry an umbrella or wear sunscreen. But every now and then, a really dangerous storm blasts in, and that's when getting accurate weather forecasts can save lives—fast and detailed warnings of what's coming and when are essential to saving lives and minimizing damage and disruption.

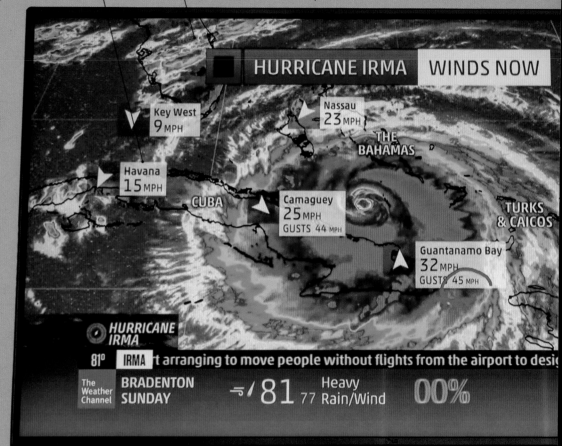

Cuba
High winds have already reached eastern Cuba.

Florida
Winds are still gentle in Florida.

Hurricane warning
When a hurricane is on its way, a warning like this might appear on your television. This shows a Doppler radar satellite image of Hurricane Irma over Cuba and approaching Florida in September 2017. The image shows where rain is falling and its intensity. Very detailed data about existing conditions gives you as much information as possible.

Pressure
The pressure at the center of the hurricane has been measured at 925 mb, indicating a very powerful hurricane.

HURRICANE IRMA   WINDS NOW

Key West 9 MPH

Nassau 23 MPH

THE BAHAMAS

Havana 15 MPH

CUBA

Camaguey 25 MPH GUSTS 44 MPH

TURKS & CAICOS

Guantanamo Bay 32 MPH GUSTS 45 MPH

HURRICANE IRMA

81° IRMA rt arranging to move people without flights from the airport to desi

The Weather Channel BRADENTON SUNDAY 81 77 Heavy Rain/Wind 00%

Storm watch
Unexpected storms can be deadly. The National Weather Service is on watch night and day to track severe weather and issue warnings as early as possible. Satellites, weather radar (Doppler), and trained storm spotters constantly scan the skies looking for clues. When they spot a storm, they try to figure out how big it will be and exactly where it will strike.

The Storm Prediction Center
Tornadoes and severe thunderstorms spring up extremely fast and the conditions that cause them often happen on a very small, local level. The Storm Prediction Center in Norman, Oklahoma, watches out for the early warning signs to spot them the second they appear.

Storm prediction staff at the NOAA

Warning center
The center sends out up-to-the-minute details of the risk of tornadoes starting. When one is on its way, they issue warnings.

Tornado alert
When a tornado is on its way, warnings go out through outdoor warning sirens, local television and radio stations, cable television systems, and NOAA Weather Radio. Most local radio and television stations broadcast storm warnings. Smartphone apps also alert people that severe weather is on the way.

Smartphone apps warn people about incoming severe weather.

WEATHER ALERT

RICANE
MA

V: 5:00 PM EDT
N:

.55 mph   CAT: 4
RE: 925 mb
: W at 12 mph
OVISORY: 11 PM EDT

IMPACTS

MPH JSTS	Sat AM-Late Sun
MPH JSTS	Sun AM
FALL	12 - 18"
ORM URGE	Up to 10 ft

FL DOT opens t

Speed of movement
The hurricane is moving at 12 mph, so you can work out when it will hit.

Watch out, Miami!
A panel tells you what to expect in Miami and when.

Tornado siren

Tornado alerts
A tornado "watch" means a tornado is probably on its way, so you need to be prepared. A tornado "warning" means a tornado has actually been spotted. You need to take cover at once.

Everyday forecasts
To tell you what the weather will be today and tomorrow, meteorologists rely on a method called "nowcasting." Supercomputers process all the observations from radar and satellites of local weather conditions. From this, they display a complete picture of the weather "now." They then project this picture 6, 12, 24, or even 48 hours ahead, giving fairly accurate forecasts.

Local knowledge
Planes need very accurate information about surface winds to take off and land safely, but normal forecasts are not so good at predicting these winds. Forecasts for airports and other places are often modified with a computer technique that uses data about local weather patterns.

Ensemble forecasts
A supercomputer has generated these accurate forecasts.

NCEP ENSEMBLE MEAN - 500mb Z (m)

NCEP ENSEMBLE 500mb Z

Longer-range forecasts
Nowadays, weather forecasters are increasingly confident with forecasts up to two weeks ahead—partly thanks to the ensemble forecasts generated by supercomputers (see pp. 136–137). These generate over 50 slightly different forecasts for the upcoming two weeks and forecasters can be confident that the weather will fall somewhere in this range.

HURRICANE TRACKING

FOLLOWING THE STORM

When a hurricane approaches, those on the ground need to know where it might strike and when. The National Hurricane Center is based in Miami, Florida, and experts there keep a continuous watch for approaching tropical storms, ready to alert the public. They also share information with weather organizations around the world. So, when Hurricane Hermine hit in 2016, the NHC was ready.

Sharing information
The National Hurricane Center provides a daily briefing to the Federal Emergency Management Agency (FEMA) about all potential and existing tropical cyclones, so that FEMA can activate any emergency measures needed.

Monitoring Hermine
When meteorologists spotted Hurricane Hermine forming from a tropical wave off Africa in 2016, the National Hurricane Center was on full alert. Hermine was the first hurricane to make landfall in Florida since Wilma in 2005, but thanks to the NHC, residents along the coasts of Florida, Georgia, and the Carolinas were prepared.

August 16–23
Meteorologists begin tracking Invest-99L, a tropical wave off the west coast of Africa. It moves off the coast, and showers and thunderstorms increase as it travels across the Atlantic Ocean.

August 24–30
The system develops a well-defined center of circulation and National Hurricane Center meteorologists are now monitoring it even more closely.

By August 25, heavy rains have spread over the Leeward Islands and reached the Greater Antilles. The wave's fast rate of travel causes gale-force winds.

At 2100 UTC on August 30, a hurricane watch is issued for part of the Big Bend coast, Florida.

August 31
Data collected by NOAA's Hurricane Hunters (see pp. 148–149) confirms the storm has reached tropical storm strength and that meteorologists are observing the development of a storm from tropical wave to a hurricane.

A storm surge warning is issued for a portion of the Gulf Coast after a Hurricane Hotline call between government weather services.

September 1
Hermine reaches the Gulf of Mexico and nears landfall.

At 1800 UTC the storm reaches hurricane intensity (measured by Air Force Reserve flights) southwest of Apalachicola, Florida. It is now a Category 1 hurricane with winds of 80 mph (130 km/h).

The National Hurricane Center director, Rick Knabb, gives a live update about Hermine on the Weather Channel.

T_1

T_2

20 km

Satellite observation
In order for storms to intensify, heat energy has to find a pathway from the ocean's surface into the atmosphere. At 4:09 p.m. on August 31, the Global Precipitation Measurement mission core satellite observed two "hot towers" in Hermine (left). These confirmed that the storm had intensified and reached tropical storm strength.

Getting ready
Emergency preparations for a hurricane may include evacuation of an area. In most cases, people protect their properties and make sure they have adequate supplies. Ahead of Hermine's arrival on land, workers in North Charleston, South Carolina, prepared sandbags for local residents.

Hermine produced **10** tornadoes, **5** in Florida, **2** in Georgia, **3** in North Carolina.

After the storm
The wind and water damage from Hermine was around $550 million, with seawater and freshwater flooding destroying homes and businesses. In Florida alone, more than 253,000 customers lost power across the state, while pecan growers in Georgia lost up to 80 percent of their crops. Two people also lost their lives.

Extratropical cyclones
When a hurricane becomes extratropical, it weakens into a large low-pressure area in which masses of cold and warm fronts produce rain, wind, and sometimes tornadoes and hail. However, winds in an extratropical cyclone are not always weaker than in the hurricane, and may even be stronger.

September 2	September 3	September 4–7	September 8
Hermine makes landfall along the Florida Big Bend coast east of St. Marks, Florida, with a 7.5-ft (2.3-m) storm surge. There are no sustained hurricane-force winds recorded as it passes over land. However, two tornadoes causing structural damage are reported in Orange County, Florida. Hermine then travels across coastal areas of Georgia, South Carolina, and North Carolina, leaving storm damage and flooding in its wake.	Hermine becomes extratropical by 1200 UTC near Oregon Inlet, North Carolina. Strong, near-hurricane force winds are recorded over the Outer Banks, barrier islands separating the Atlantic Ocean from the mainland. The sustained winds measure up to 71 mph (114 km/h) with gusts of up to 84 mph (135 km/h).	The storm moves eastward over the Atlantic Ocean away from the coast and maintains 69-mph (111-km/h) winds until September 5. Now an occluded low, the storm weakens and turns northwest, moving closer to the coast again. By September 7, it is traveling offshore of New Jersey and Long Island.	The weakened low, with winds that have dropped below gale force, moves northeast and dissipates soon after 1800 UTC near Chatham, Massachusetts.

A storm surge hits Massachusetts on March 3, 2018.

A storm surge batters the coast of Long Island, New York.

Monitoring landfall
The evening before Hermine made landfall, US Geological Survey (USGS) scientists installed storm-tide sensors and barometric pressure monitoring devices along the Big Bend coast. They put them on bridges, piers, and other structures likely to survive. The readings were used to assess storm damage and create computer models for future flooding.

Storm surges and coastal areas
A major cause of damage, storm surges happen when hurricanes make landfall. They are a combination of the rise of sea level because of the low pressure, high winds, and high waves, and can cause major flooding and sometimes loss of life, see above left. Even when Hermine was weakening, it caused very rough seas off the coast of Long Island (above right).

HURRICANE HUNTERS

ROLLERCOASTER RIDE

NOAA's Hurricane Hunter aircraft are high-flying weather stations. Other planes change course to avoid storms, but Hurricane Hunters fly near or through storms to study them. The crews risk their lives. Surrounded by dense cloud and buffeted by heavy rains and high winds, they have to use radar to plot their course. But their data is vital, helping to predict where a hurricane will hit, and how severe it will be.

Bumpy ride
The NOAA Lockheed WP-3D Orion N42RF, also known as "Kermit," has an onboard radar system that measures wind and rain. It can be in the air for about eight hours, but it's a bumpy ride, everything inside—even pencils— must be fixed in place to cope with the shaking and swaying.

Two-of-a-kind
There's one other aircraft like this in existence, nicknamed "Miss Piggy."

First into the eye
Manned flights into hurricanes began July 27, 1943, when, as a bet with his trainees, Lt. Col. Joseph Duckworth, with Ralph O'Hair as copilot, flew his AT-6 *Texan* into a Category 1 storm near Galveston, Texas. He was the first person intentionally to fly through the eye of a hurricane.

Studying the storm
Missions begin with a low-level flight to observe the weather system from the outside. Once it has become a tropical storm or hurricane, the plane climbs to a higher altitude, where crews fly through the eye five to six times to locate the low-pressure center, and release dropsondes.

Dropsonde
A dropsonde is designed to be dropped out of an aircraft to collect atmospheric data, which it then sends back the aircraft. The dropsonde usually contains a GPS receiver that can detect wind speed and wind direction as well as pressure, temperature, and humidity sensors that all capture data. A parachute at the top helps it float safely back down to Earth.

Type of aircraft:
Gulfstream IV

Height: 45,000 ft (13,715 m)

Where flown: around the periphery of a storm

Type of aircraft:
P-3 Hurricane Hunter

Height: 5,000–10,000 ft (1,525–3,050 m)

Where flown: into the eye of the storm

Type of aircraft:
Raytheon Coyote drone

Height: 200–5,000 ft (60–1,525 m)

Where flown: gathers data from low altitudes

Type of aircraft:
Global Hawk drone

Height: 60,000 ft (1,830 m)

Where flown: gathers data from high altitudes

Aircraft and probes
Hurricane hunting is changing. For more than seven decades, brave crews flown into monster storms, but in 2014, scientists successfully deployed a drone, from an aircraft, into a hurricane above the Atlantic. These remote-controlled machines are likely to become the future of this type of weather watching.

Help from space

Monitoring hurricanes is a team effort. While Hurricane Hunters gather unique data from the center of the storm, satellites can also provide useful hurricane data. They can track its path and see what other weather conditions may also be coming. Metereologists need as much data as they can get.

Image capture

Images are taken by a variety of instruments on board these aircraft and the data transferred via satellite to the NHC and others.

Doppler x-band radar in the tail scans vertically and horizontally.

Engines
The WP-3D has four engines and is a modified version of a military aircraft.

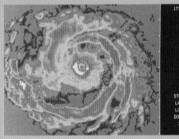

There is c-band radar in both the lower fuselage and nose.

Mission crew

Every mission has a pilot and copilot, a navigator to decide the flight plan, route, and altitude, an aerial reconnaissance weather officer who, as flight director, continuously monitors atmospheric data and sends it to the National Hurricane Center, and a weather loadmaster who checks the systems and deploys dropsondes as needed.

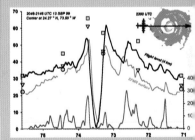

Stepped frequency microwave radiometers measure wind speed and rain.

The pilot and copilot inside the cockpit of a Hurricane Hunter aircraft

Inside the the eye

A Lockheed WP-3D Orion flies inside the eye of Hurricane Katrina on August 28, 2005 (see pp. 90–91). The wind is usually strongest around the eye, but the center of the eye is normally calm. By 11:00 a.m. on August 28, the center of this storm was about 225 miles (360 km) from the mouth of the Mississippi River. Residents in its path were advised to evacuate immediately.

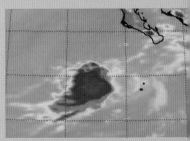

This infrared image of Tropical Storm Frank was taken by the Global Hawk drone.

A new era in meteorology

The Director of Operations at the National Environmental Satellite Center studies the first-ever satellite map, a composite of 450 photos, showing weather conditions around the world on February 13, 1965. The "First Complete View of the World's Weather" was made with information from the TIROS-9 weather satellite, the first to be placed in a near-polar orbit. TIROS-9 was an 18-sided prism with 21 batteries powered by about 9,000 silicon solar cells. It took pictures of Earth's cloud cover with two wide-angle TV cameras.

FIRST COMPLETE VIEW OF THE WORLD'S WEA

TIROS IX

THROUGH HISTORY

"Red sky at night, sailors' delight; Red sky in the morning, sailors take warning." In the last 50 or so years we have developed state-of-the-art weather tools to forecast our weather, but before that people had to make do with less reliable ways of predicting the weather. However, even as far back as 300 BCE some people were ahead of the curve when it came to understanding and tracking the weather.

1570 drawing of an aurora, depicted as candles in the sky.

US Navy biplane in 1934 with meteorograph on starboard wing

The Chinese calendar
By 300 BCE, Chinese astronomers had divided the year into 24 festivals, each associated with a different type of weather. These types were created to reflect changes in climate, which farmers used to help regulate their agricultural activities.

"Little cold" from the Chinese solar calendar

Space weather
English astronomer Edmund Halley is probably best known for the comet that is named for him. However, in 1716, he suggested that auroras are caused by magnetic space particles moving along Earth's magnetic field lines. He was a pioneer in this field and his studies of geomagnetism revolutionized the way that scientists thought about Earth. The auroras at the North and South Poles had been observed for centuries, but Halley was the first to connect the auroras to Earth's magnetic field.

Early weather watching
It was obvious that weather forms in the sky, so early researchers sent kites and balloons high into the atmosphere. The balloons were fitted with a meteorograph, a device for recording things such as air pressure, temperature, and moisture. The invention of the airplane in 1903 made the skies more accessible.

Hurricane tracking
In a letter written to Queen Isabella of Spain in 1494, the explorer Christopher Columbus gave the first European account of a hurricane in the Atlantic Ocean, south of Cuba. On a later voyage in 1502, he recognized signs of an approaching "huracan" storm, and sought shelter for his ships until it had passed. Three of the four ships still broke their anchor lines and were driven before the waves, but they all survived because of his quick thinking.

TIROS

Weather map of tropical storm Alice

Naming storms
Hurricanes have been given names for centuries, but they often caused confusion, so a better system was needed in order to maintain more accurate records. In 1953, the US began using female names for tropical cyclones, starting with Alice. The naming is now strictly controlled by the World Meteorological Organization, and since 1979 both male and female names have been used to identify the storms. The first male name used was Bob.

Operator plotting aircraft in WW II

Finding new uses
In World War II, radar systems were used by all sides to guide missions and track aircraft. When the war ended, weather services around the world started using radar to measure the position and intensity of precipitation.

First weather satellite
On April 1, 1960, TIROS-1, the first successful low-Earth orbital weather satellite, was launched. It operated for only 78 days, but sent enough accurate data to prove that Earth's cloud cover and weather patterns could be monitored from space, providing accurate data.

ALL-YEAR

WEATHER

CLIMATE ZONES
WHERE WOULD YOU RATHER LIVE?

Everywhere in the world has its own typical weather that it gets most of the time. You're never going to go sunbathing in the Arctic or build a snowman in the Amazon rain forest! Although every day is different, and sometimes weather can go from one extreme to another in a matter of hours, a region's typical weather, averaged out over 30 or more years, is known as its "climate"—how warm or cold, wet or dry it is most of the time. What's the climate like where you are?

Earth's climate zones

The warmest, tropical climates are on either side of the equator where the Sun is strong. The coldest are at the poles, where the Sun is weak. In between sits the temperate zone, with warm summers and cool winters. Within each of these zones, inland climates are drier and more extreme, whereas coastal climates are more moist and mild. Many climate classification schemes, like this one, are influenced by the natural vegetation that grows in a given place.

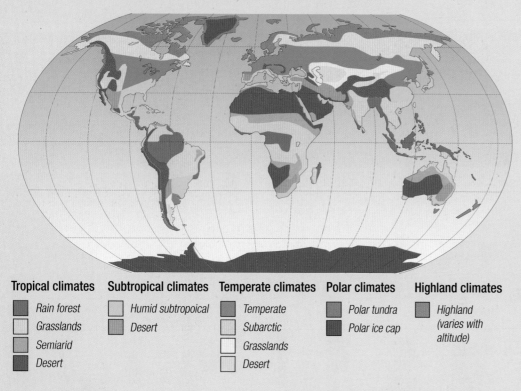

Tropical climates	Subtropical climates	Temperate climates	Polar climates	Highland climates
Rain forest	Humid subtropoical	Temperate	Polar tundra	Highland (varies with altitude)
Grasslands	Desert	Subarctic	Polar ice cap	
Semiarid		Grasslands		
Desert		Desert		

Weather tells you **what to wear** each day. **Climate** tells you what to have **in your closet!**

POLAR
COLD AS ICE

Brr! Polar climates are bitterly cold! In winter, it's dark for months, and chill winds whip across ice and snow. Even in summer, when it's light all the time, it stays below 50 °F (10 °C) and the tundra revealed where snow melts is bleak and treeless.

TEMPERATE
GO WITH THE SEASONS

Misty, colorful autumns, cool winters, blustery springs and warm summers—there's rarely a day the same in the temperate zone. No wonder people love talking about weather! But it's all mostly mild compared to the polar chill and tropical heat either side.

TROPICAL
PARADISE FOR VACATIONS

You won't often get cold in tropical climates! It's warm all year under the strong tropical Sun. But you can get soaked in super-wet places, or parched in scorching deserts. In many places, it pours with rain for half the year, while the other half is dry as bone.

POLAR CLIMATES

Polar tundra: Very cold, dry winters and mild summers

Polar ice caps: Icy, with temperatures below freezing all year-round

TEMPERATE CLIMATES

Temperate: Four seasons with chilly winters

Subarctic: Long, cold winters and mild summers

Grasslands: Hot, dry summers and cold winters

Desert: Dry with cold winters

TROPICAL CLIMATES

Rain forest: Very warm and wet year-round

Tropical grassland: A wet season with high rainfall and a dry season with very little rainfall

Humid subtropical: Warm summers and mild winters

Deserts: Very dry, with less than 10 in (25.4 cm) of rainfall a year

Climate control

Lots of factors affect how different climates exist around the world. Here are a few of them.

Sunlight
Sunshine gives warmth. It hits the tropics strongest, creating the warm tropical climates. Its intensity also moves north and south and back again over the year, which creates seasons.

Oceans
Oceans give moisture to coastal climates, making them wetter. They also take longer to heat up and cool down than land, which moderates climate swings. That's why coastal climates are far more moderate than those of continental interiors.

Currents
Ocean currents carry cool and warm water over huge distances and have a major influence on the weather. Northwest Europe would be much cooler without the warm North Atlantic current flowing eastward around the coasts.

Mountains
Air gets colder higher up, so mountain climates are chilly, often with snow. They're also wetter because they get in the way of rain clouds. They rob winds of their moisture, making the slopes on the leeside (away from the wind) much drier.

Winds
In every region, there are typical or "prevailing" winds (see p. 41). In temperate regions, rain-bearing westerly winds make the west sides of continents much damper.

Forests
Forests add moisture to the air and shade the ground, keeping the climate more moderate. They also absorb carbon dioxide, reducing the greenhouse effect.

Deserts

Phew! 113°F (45°C) and rising. That's a typical day in the Sahara, the world's largest hot desert. Clear skies mean the temperature drops over 77°F (25°C) at night, but the Sahara's summer days are truly scorching. In the tropics, most deserts are on the west side of continents where the easterly winds blow farthest over the land. The biggest and hottest are also linked to the global weather circulation.

It's all to do with the Hadley Cell. The Hadley Cell circulation sees warm air rising at the equator, drifting toward the poles, cooling and sinking. As it sinks, it's like a blow-dryer for the air. Sinking air is very stable. It's also super dry and clear. Naturally, deserts form where the Hadley Cell has its downward arm, in the subtropics. There's a belt of them right around the world. Clouds are very rare and rainfall even rarer. It does rain every now and then but it's erratic and short-lived, and water quickly evaporates.

Desert animals have developed ingenious ways to survive in the big heat. The Namib desert beetle harvests moisture from fog and dew. It's condensed on the beetle's bumpy back and funneled right into its mouth. Worryingly, though, the Sahara has expanded by well over 10 percent over the last century, making life hard for people and animals on the desert fringes. Climate change is not only intensifying the Hadley Cell, it seems, but making it stretch farther toward the poles.

EL NIÑO

A GUEST FOR CHRISTMAS

Every three to seven years, there's a dramatic shift in Pacific weather patterns. Usually, tropical winds blow away westward from South America, pushing warm water with them. But in an El Niño event, this reverses. The winds weaken or even blow east, letting warm water drift back east, and triggering storms and floods in the Americas. Then, before settling down, it often bounces back too much as a La Niña, bringing floods to Australia and droughts to the Americas.

Changing history

Historians believe that the conquest of the Incas of Peru by the Spanish Conquistadores may have been aided by the El Niño of 1532. When the Spanish leader, Francisco Pizarro (right), sailed down the Peruvian coast, his ships benefited from its northeasterly winds.

The El Niño effect

This 3D image of cloud and surface temperatures came from data supplied by the Terra satellite. It shows a well-developed El Niño, with the warm water (red) sitting off the coast of Peru and Ecuador in western South America. El Niño gets its name from the Spanish term for the Christ Child, because it often comes at Christmas-time.

Fishing trawler

Warmer waters may bleach coral and kill off the reef

Disadvantages and benefits

El Niño certainly brings many problems, but there are also advantages. In El Niño years, there are warmer-than-average temperatures across most of southern Australia. The increased heat leads to bleached coral reefs, drought, destructive bushfires, and a higher risk of cyclones. However, warmer waters also attract many more fish, making it a great time for the fishing industry.

Storm systems lead to surging waves and terrible flooding.

Tropical storms

In El Niño years, the warm water in the eastern Pacific piles up thunderstorms, dumping rains far inland in the Americas. More hurricanes are generated in the eastern Pacific but less in the Atlantic, Gulf of Mexico, and the Caribbean.

Flooding

El Niño triggers severe weather on the western coasts of South America that frequently brings flooding and devastating landslides (left) to Peru, Bolivia, northern Chile, and northern Argentina. During the 1997 to 1998 El Niño, Peru suffered massive flooding that caused over $3.5 billion worth of damage to buildings and farmlands.

Forest fires

El Niño can produce drought in Africa, India, Indonesia, Australia, and the Americas. In forested areas, this creates the perfect conditions for raging forest fires that destroy plants and animals, as well as threatening towns and villages. It seems that our warming climate is making El Niño more intense, and these "super" El Niños will magnify the effects.

Unpredictable

In complete contrast to the destruction caused by floods, fire, and drought, El Niño's plentiful rains in spring and summer along the coasts of southern Brazil and Argentina can help the farmers sow and raise their crops. However, El Niño and La Niña are unpredictable, so farmers have had to learn to be adaptable to changing weather conditions.

Paired events

The combination of El Niño and La Niña is called the El Niño Southern Oscillation (ENSO). El Niño is called the warming phases, because the eastern Pacific warms up. La Niña is described as the cooling phase, because the eastern Pacific cools. They each usually last 9–12 months, but some may last for years, upsetting weather.

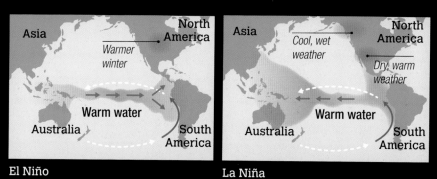

El Niño

La Niña

MONSOONS

LIFE-GIVING AND LIFE-TAKING WINDS

In many parts of the tropics, there are just two seasons; a half-year-long dry season when little or no rain falls, and a half-year-long wet season when rain comes down in torrents. "Monsoon" is the name for the wind that causes this seasonal variation, and also for the heavy rains themselves. People in this part of the world rely on the monsoon rains, which are a vital relief from the drought—but if they arrive too late, or fall too heavily, they can also bring disaster.

Monsoon maker
The Asian monsoon happens partly because of the movement of the Sun's hottest zone, the Intertropical Convergence Zone (ITCZ, see p. 42), to the south and north of the equator and back again during the year.

Welcoming the rain
Billions of people around the globe depend on monsoon rains for their yearly rainfall. In 2018, the monsoons brought 91 percent of India's rainfall. The coming of the monsoons is celebrated. The weather is generally warm, and after a long period of drought, a downpour is something of a relief.

Where in the world
The Indian monsoon is probably the best known, but monsoons happen all over southern Asia and Australasia. They also happen in West Africa, and some scientists assert in the southern USA and South America as well.

Driving in a monsoon, Phuket, Thailand

Key
NH Summer Monsoon
NH Winter Monsoon
SH Summer Monsoon
SH Winter Monsoon

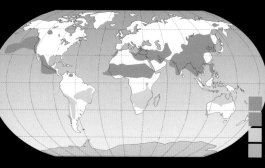

Houses in Benin, Africa, are built on stilts to escap monsoon rains

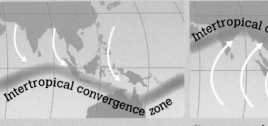
Intertropical convergence zone

Intertropical convergence zone

Happy cows
Rice, tea, and dairy farming in India rely on the summer monsoon for their water. The winds also drive hydroelectric power plants. The name "monsoon" comes from the Arabic word "mausim" meaning a shift in season or wind.

Winter drought
In the northern hemisphere winter, the overhead Sun moves south of the equator, and with it goes the ITCZ. Winds are drawn behind it, blowing southeasterly off the Asian continent, before veering southwest as they cross the equator. Blowing off the land, these winds become very dry, causing drought.

Summer rain
In the northern hemisphere summer, the ITCZ migrates back north, until by June it is moving far up over India. It draws with it warm winds, which pick up moisture over the ocean and then drop it in deluges wherever they meet warm air rising over hot land. The wet season lasts until the ITCZ heads back south again.

Record monsoon floods
Some of the world's heaviest rain is carried onto land by monsoon winds. They can cost people their homes, and sometimes their lives. Cherrapunji, India, holds the 48-hour rainfall world record with 98.15 ins (2,493 mm) on June 15–16, 1995.

2011
China
300+ killed and missing, 12 million displaced

2014
Malaysia
24 killed and missing 200,000 displaced

2015
South India
200+ people killed and missing, 1.8 million displaced

2017
India, Bangladesh, and Nepal
1,200+ people killed and missing 40 million displaced

2018
Southern India
600+ people killed and missing, 5 million+ displaced

ANCIENT PUZZLE

CLUES TO OUR PAST

Ever wondered what Earth's climate was like millions of years ago? Like detectives investigating a mystery, scientists called paleoclimatologists search for evidence of what conditions were like on Earth long ago. From tell-tale clues in the landscape, animal and plant remains, and layers of ice, they build up a picture of the planet's past climate. The more we know about our climate's history (see pp.172–175), the better we will understand how it might change in the future.

Preserved rain craters
Ancient rain falling on sand made these little craters, which were preserved as the sand turned to rock. By calculating the raindrops' size, scientists learn about the air pressure and the density of the atmosphere at the time.

Ice ages

An ice age is a period of cold global temperatures, when much of Earth is covered by ice. During each ice age there are several very cold spells, known as "glacial maxima," broken by warmer periods called "interglacials." There have been five main ice ages.

Huronian 2,400–2,100 mya	**Cryogenian** 850–635 mya	**Andean–Saharan** 460–430 mya	**Karoo** 360–260 mya	**Quaternary** 2.6 mya–the present
Lack of volcanic activity, reduced the atmosphere's CO₂ levels, and, as a result, its temperature. The only life was single-cell organisms.	*Described as "Snowball Earth," because it is thought that the whole planet was frozen and ice sheets may have reached the equator.*	*This ice age was marked by a mass extinction, the second-most severe in Earth's history. At the end of this ice age, simple plants evolved.*	*Plants colonizing Earth took in CO₂ and released oxygen, reducing the greenhouse effect (see p. 22) and triggering a new ice age.*	*Humans emerged and developed. This ice age is ongoing: We are in a warm interglacial that began about 10,000 years ago.*

Ice coring

Air bubbles trapped in ice sheets and glaciers can reveal the makeup of Earth's atmosphere in past ages. To find these bubbles, scientists drill out cylindrical samples, or cores, of ice. They compare the amounts of carbon dioxide and methane in the air bubbles with the levels of the gases in today's atmosphere. The deepest ice core samples are from more than 2 miles (3 km) below the surface in Antarctica and Greenland; the oldest date back 800,000 years.

This scientist is using an auger to drill a shallow core from an ice pack in Antarctica.

Ice Age beetle

In 2014, scientists digging at a bog in Slotseng, Denmark, discovered insects, including the beetle *Thanatophilus dispar* (left), from 14,000 years ago. The scientists looked at the temperature ranges in the places where the same insects can still be found. They concluded that Denmark's summer temperatures 14,000 years ago were similar to what they are now, but that in winter it fell to 1.4°F (−17°C)—much lower than today's average winter temperatures.

Coral data

Paleoclimatologists can date the remains of ancient tropical corals by measuring the radioactive decay (breakdown) of uranium in their fossils. Finding and dating coral fossils in a place shows that the site was under a tropical sea at a specific time in the past. What's more, the chemicals in the chalky skeletons of fossil corals show how their growth was affected by climate changes such as variations in temperature or rainfall.

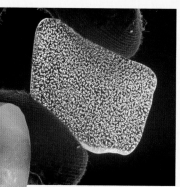

This sliver of Antarctic ice shows tiny bubbles of air trapped when the ice formed hundreds or even thousands of years ago.

The dark band in this ice core from Antarctica is a layer of volcanic ash that settled on the ice sheet around 21,000 years ago.

Underground evidence

Stalactites and stalagmites in caves can reveal much about the weather on the surface at the time that they formed. These spectacular structures grow as water trickling through the cave roof deposits layers of minerals. Slice one through and you see the layers as growth rings. Narrow rings tell of a drier climate, wider rings of wetter spells. There is also chemical evidence: oxygen isotopes (different forms of oxygen) in a layer can show if it formed in an ice age; carbon isotopes give clues to the extent of plant cover at the time.

More clues

There are many natural sources of information about Earth's ancient climate. Each is a small piece of the jigsaw that reveals the full picture.

Some rocks formed from desert sand, others from silt washed out of glaciers.

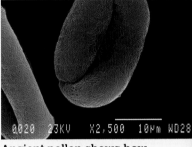

Ancient pollen shows how plant communties changed as the climate altered.

Growth rings on tree trunks are wider during warmer, wetter years.

Fossil plankton: These tiny marine organisms thrive in times with warmer seas.

OCEAN CURRENTS

SPREADING HEAT

Ocean currents are the world's great heat spreaders. Without them, Britain would be as chilly as Alaska, and California would scorch like the Sahara. Ocean currents send warmth from tropical regions and help them cool off, and bring cooling waters from the poles to the tropics. Outside the equatorial belt, ocean currents are perhaps the main driver of weather patterns.

Coral Beach,
Isle of Skye, Scotland

Surface currents

There are two kinds of currents in the ocean. First, on the surface there are fast currents driven by winds. These currents create five great loops or gyres, which flow clockwise in the northern hemisphere and anticlockwise in the southern hemisphere. They are driven westward in the tropics by trade winds, then back eastward in the midlatitudes by westerly winds.

Surface currents flow clockwise (blue) or anticlockwise (red) according to their latitude.

Deep currents

Deep down, the ocean is moving, too, driven by differences in water density. Indeed, the whole ocean is slowly turning over, like a giant conveyor belt. Starting with chilly waters sinking in the Arctic, it spirals through all the oceans, taking six centuries to complete its amazing world trip. Without this continual heat circulation, the world's climate would be much more extreme, with superhot tropics and icy midlatitudes.

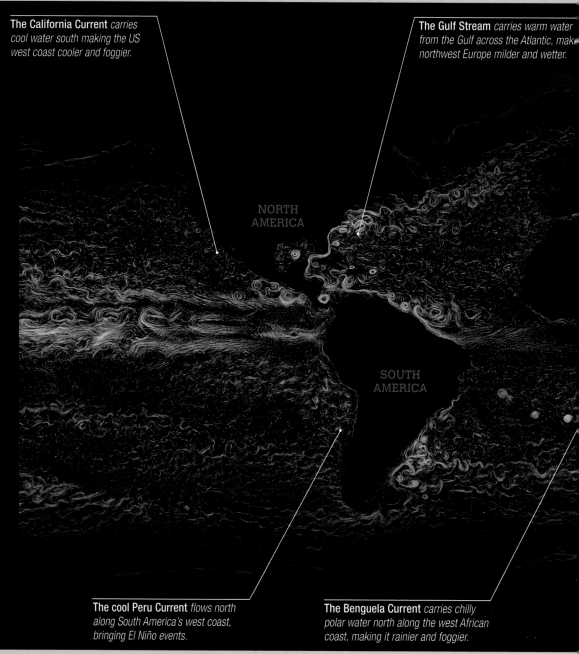

The California Current *carries cool water south making the US west coast cooler and foggier.*

The Gulf Stream *carries warm water from the Gulf across the Atlantic, making northwest Europe milder and wetter.*

NORTH AMERICA

SOUTH AMERICA

The cool Peru Current *flows north along South America's west coast, bringing El Niño events.*

The Benguela Current *carries chilly polar water north along the west African coast, making it rainier and foggier.*

The Gulf Stream

The Gulf Stream is like a central heating system, carrying warm tropical water from the Gulf of Mexico, northward past Florida, right up the east coast of the US, and then across the Atlantic. Thanks to the Gulf Stream, the west coast of Britain and Ireland enjoy mild waters. But, if global warming melts the Arctic ice, it could flood the North Atlantic and stall the Gulf Stream's flow.

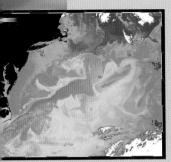

e Gulf Stream is shown in red

Cool Benguela

Ocean currents have a major influence on clouds and rain. The Benguela Current is the eastern loop of the South Atlantic, a cool current carrying an Antarctic chill up the west coast of Africa. When southwesterly winds blow over it and onland, it produces fog. Persistent fogs bring moisture to the Namib Desert, but are a hazard for ships.

OCEAN CURRENT SPEEDS

4 mph (6.6 km/h): The average speed of the Gulf Stream

150 times: The number of times more water than the Amazon River carried by the Gulf Stream

100 times: The number of times more water than the Amazon River moved by the deep ocean conveyor

1000 years: The time it takes for water to complete its global journey by the deep ocean conveyor

8 percent: The proportion of the oceans moved by surface currents

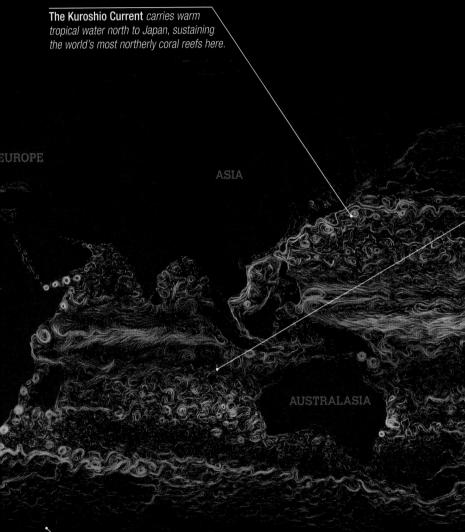

The Kuroshio Current carries warm tropical water north to Japan, sustaining the world's most northerly coral reefs here.

EUROPE

ASIA

AUSTRALASIA

Whales and sharks **follow currents** to and from **where they feed**.

The South Equatorial Current flows westwards along the equator in all major oceans, driven by trade winds

Keeping the conveyor moving

As scientists monitor the seas south of Greenland, they're seeing a slowdown of the deep ocean conveyor as it leaves to flow south. This is the one place, apart from Antarctica, where waters are dense enough to sink and get the conveyor going. But there is a flood of fresh water due to ice melting on land coming through the crucial Fram Strait. Fresh water just isn't heavy enough to sink in salt water, and if water doesn't sink, the conveyor stops, with worrying consequences for our climate.

Very sadly, pollutants in the sea may be carried on currents far and wide, including to polar bears's homes in the Arctic.

The Circumpolar Current flows very strongly from west to east right around Antartica, helping keep its weather separate.

Arctic chill

How do you survive and thrive in one of the most challenging climates on the planet?

In the Canadian Arctic and Greenland, traditional Inuit homes are some of the best and most famous examples of how humans have lived in the harshest of climates in the smartest of ways.

Domed snowhouses for winter living have possibly been built for 1,000 years or more (this photo dates to 1924). Fine, compact snow is dug out and shaped with a snow knife, snow blocks are laid in a circle, and the tops trimmed to begin a spiral. The natural insulation of the snow conserves heat inside very well. Drafts are kept out by a sealskin flap over a tunneled entrance.

Fewer Inuit live in snowhouses nowadays, but they are still used during hunting trips. An experienced Inuit builder can build a snow igloo in between one and two hours. "Igloo" is the Inuit word for house. So you live in an igloo, too.

Chasing the Sun

Seasonal changes in oxygen levels make many fish, crustaceans, and mollusks relocate higher or lower in the water columns of seas and lakes. However, in a saltwater lake in Eil Malk Island, Palau, in the western Pacific, some extraordinary golden jellyfish migrate for unique reasons. Every day around 600,000 of them circle the lake repeatedly, tracking the Sun's movement across the sky. The jellyfish have algae living in their tissues, and they swim around to ensure the algae gets enough sunlight for photosynthesis. In return, the algae give the jellyfish energy and nutrients.

ON THE MOVE

Some of the most epic of all animal journeys are those of migrating animals; animals who journey with the seasons to find better weather and more food. In vast numbers, they navigate with extraordinary precision, and overcome steep odds and severe obstacles. Studying the changes in the migration habits of animals can help us understand the effect that our changing climate is having on the animal kingdom.

Red crabs have right of way

Safety in numbers

In winter, snow geese travel south in flocks of up to 1,000 birds from their breeding grounds in and around the Arctic to warmer coastal areas of the US. Similarly, an African wildebeest herd may have as many as two million animals as they migrate to follow the rains.

Snow geese

African wildebeest

Island travelers

Every year, about 50 million red crabs emerge from the forests of Christmas Island in the Indian Ocean and head toward the beach. The spring migration is triggered by the start of the wet season. Males and females mate and females release the eggs into the ocean. Mom and Dad head back to the forest, and the juveniles join them a few weeks later.

Arctic tern

Following the rains

The wandering glider dragonfly is also called the globe skimmer as it travels from India to Africa and back again, up to 11,000 miles (18,000 km). Four generations of these insects move from the monsoon season in India to the rainy season in Africa in the longest-ever insect migration.

Wandering glider dragonfly

Brumation

Sometimes cold-blooded animals brumate, or enter a hibernation-like state, to survive. Individual garter snakes will migrate large distances from their foraging habitats to reach communal sites called *hibernacula*. In cold climates, sometimes thousands of them winter together in dens, protected from freezing and deadly temperatures.

Humpback whale

Finding the Sun

The Adélie is the smallest species of penguin in the Antarctic. These hardy little birds breed in colonies that can number many thousands along the Antarctic coastline in the warmer summer months. They are highly sensitive to temperature changes, and during the winter they follow the Sun to migrate north where it's warmer. Some travel up to 10,940 miles (17,600 km) during their migration.

Adélie penguins

Garter snakes emerging from their winter den

Long migrations

Two amazing animal travelers are the Arctic tern and the humpback whale. Moving between Greenland and Antarctica, the longest migratory bird achieves a round trip of 50,000 miles (over 80,000 km). The humpback makes one of the longest migrations of any mammal, traveling up to 10,000 miles (16,400 km) from breeding to feeding grounds and back again.

CLIMATE

CHAOS

CLIMATE TIMELINE

CHANGING EARTH

Earth's climate is always changing. It has been far colder, and far warmer, at times in the past. But Earth's atmosphere has become 2.07°F (1.15°C) warmer since 1880, and most of this has happened only in the last few decades.

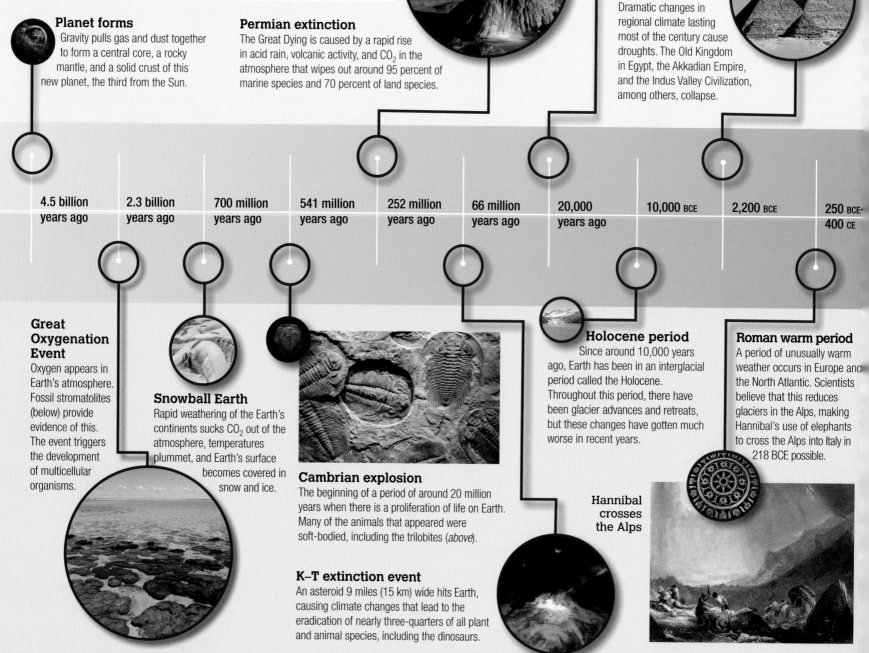

Glacier, Argentina

Icy Earth
This is the time during the Last Glacial Period when ice sheets are at their greatest extent. Vast ice sheets cover northern Europe and Asia, while an ice sheet more than 1 mile (1.6 km) thick covers much of North America.

4.2 Kiloyear Event
Dramatic changes in regional climate lasting most of the century cause droughts. The Old Kingdom in Egypt, the Akkadian Empire, and the Indus Valley Civilization, among others, collapse.

Planet forms
Gravity pulls gas and dust together to form a central core, a rocky mantle, and a solid crust of this new planet, the third from the Sun.

Permian extinction
The Great Dying is caused by a rapid rise in acid rain, volcanic activity, and CO_2 in the atmosphere that wipes out around 95 percent of marine species and 70 percent of land species.

4.5 billion years ago	2.3 billion years ago	700 million years ago	541 million years ago	252 million years ago	66 million years ago	20,000 years ago	10,000 BCE	2,200 BCE	250 BCE– 400 CE

Great Oxygenation Event
Oxygen appears in Earth's atmosphere. Fossil stromatolites (below) provide evidence of this. The event triggers the development of multicellular organisms.

Snowball Earth
Rapid weathering of the Earth's continents sucks CO_2 out of the atmosphere, temperatures plummet, and Earth's surface becomes covered in snow and ice.

Cambrian explosion
The beginning of a period of around 20 million years when there is a proliferation of life on Earth. Many of the animals that appeared were soft-bodied, including the trilobites (above).

K–T extinction event
An asteroid 9 miles (15 km) wide hits Earth, causing climate changes that lead to the eradication of nearly three-quarters of all plant and animal species, including the dinosaurs.

Holocene period
Since around 10,000 years ago, Earth has been in an interglacial period called the Holocene. Throughout this period, there have been glacier advances and retreats, but these changes have gotten much worse in recent years.

Hannibal crosses the Alps

Roman warm period
A period of unusually warm weather occurs in Europe and the North Atlantic. Scientists believe that this reduces glaciers in the Alps, making Hannibal's use of elephants to cross the Alps into Italy in 218 BCE possible.

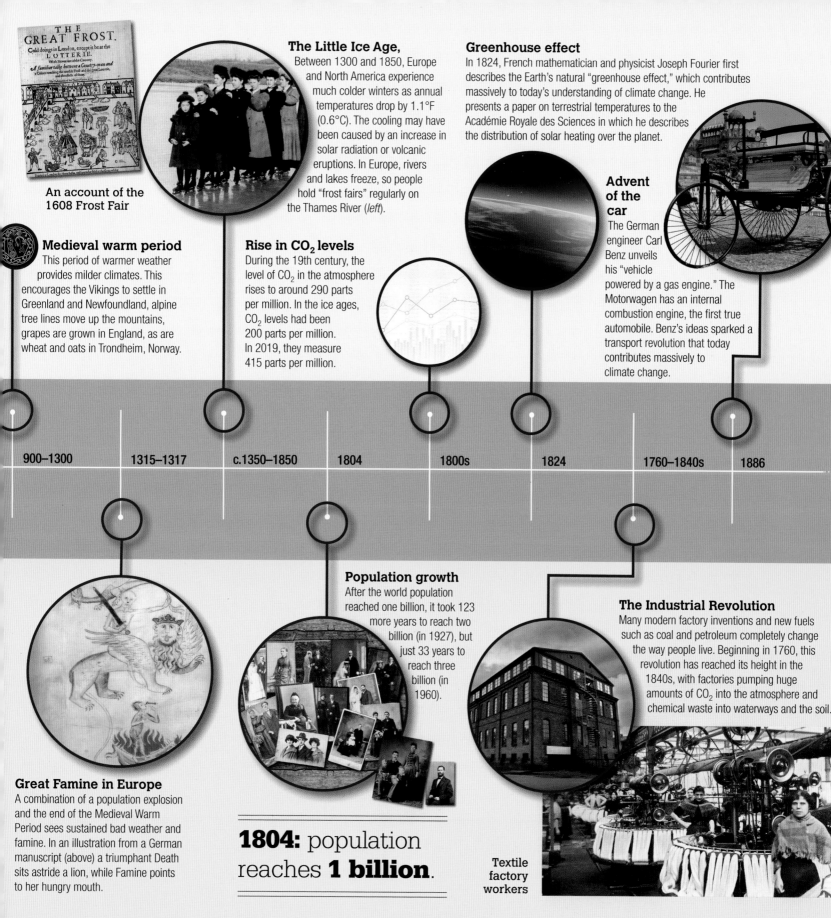

An account of the 1608 Frost Fair

THE GREAT FROST. Cold doings in London, except it be at the LOTTERIE.

The Little Ice Age,

Between 1300 and 1850, Europe and North America experience much colder winters as annual temperatures drop by 1.1°F (0.6°C). The cooling may have been caused by an increase in solar radiation or volcanic eruptions. In Europe, rivers and lakes freeze, so people hold "frost fairs" regularly on the Thames River (*left*).

Greenhouse effect

In 1824, French mathematician and physicist Joseph Fourier first describes the Earth's natural "greenhouse effect," which contributes massively to today's understanding of climate change. He presents a paper on terrestrial temperatures to the Académie Royale des Sciences in which he describes the distribution of solar heating over the planet.

Advent of the car

The German engineer Carl Benz unveils his "vehicle powered by a gas engine." The Motorwagen has an internal combustion engine, the first true automobile. Benz's ideas sparked a transport revolution that today contributes massively to climate change.

Medieval warm period

This period of warmer weather provides milder climates. This encourages the Vikings to settle in Greenland and Newfoundland, alpine tree lines move up the mountains, grapes are grown in England, as are wheat and oats in Trondheim, Norway.

Rise in CO_2 levels

During the 19th century, the level of CO_2 in the atmosphere rises to around 290 parts per million. In the ice ages, CO_2 levels had been 200 parts per million. In 2019, they measure 415 parts per million.

| 900–1300 | 1315–1317 | c.1350–1850 | 1804 | 1800s | 1824 | 1760–1840s | 1886 |

Population growth

After the world population reached one billion, it took 123 more years to reach two billion (in 1927), but just 33 years to reach three billion (in 1960).

The Industrial Revolution

Many modern factory inventions and new fuels such as coal and petroleum completely change the way people live. Beginning in 1760, this revolution has reached its height in the 1840s, with factories pumping huge amounts of CO_2 into the atmosphere and chemical waste into waterways and the soil.

Great Famine in Europe

A combination of a population explosion and the end of the Medieval Warm Period sees sustained bad weather and famine. In an illustration from a German manuscript (above) a triumphant Death sits astride a lion, while Famine points to her hungry mouth.

1804: population reaches **1 billion**.

Textile factory workers

1927: population reaches 2 billion.

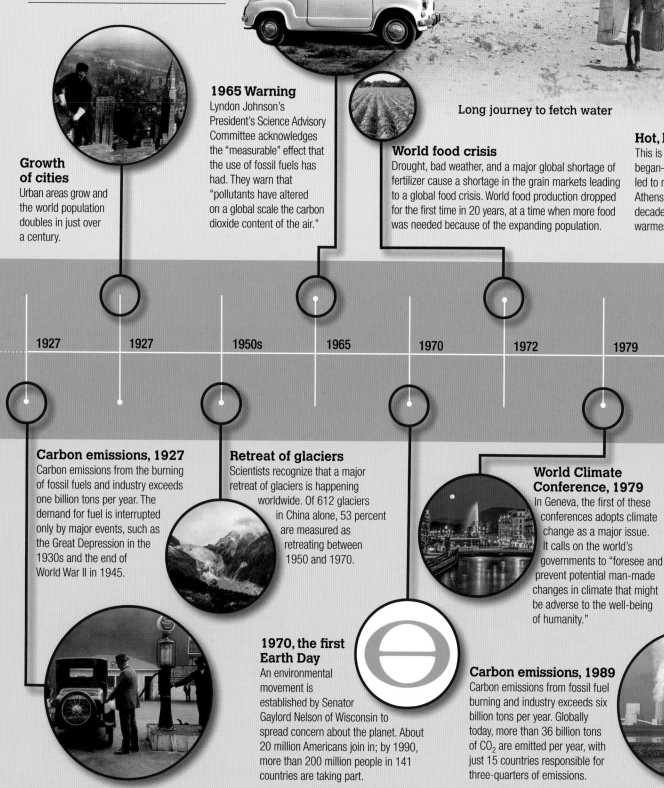

Growth of cities
Urban areas grow and the world population doubles in just over a century.

1965 Warning
Lyndon Johnson's President's Science Advisory Committee acknowledges the "measurable" effect that the use of fossil fuels has had. They warn that "pollutants have altered on a global scale the carbon dioxide content of the air."

Long journey to fetch water

World food crisis
Drought, bad weather, and a major global shortage of fertilizer cause a shortage in the grain markets leading to a global food crisis. World food production dropped for the first time in 20 years, at a time when more food was needed because of the expanding population.

Hot, hot, hot
This is the warmest year since records began—a prolonged heat wave in Greece led to more than 1,000 deaths around Athens alone. The 1980s is the hottest decade on record, with seven of the eight warmest years recorded up to 1990.

| 1927 | 1927 | 1950s | 1965 | 1970 | 1972 | 1979 | 1987 | 1989 |

Carbon emissions, 1927
Carbon emissions from the burning of fossil fuels and industry exceeds one billion tons per year. The demand for fuel is interrupted only by major events, such as the Great Depression in the 1930s and the end of World War II in 1945.

Retreat of glaciers
Scientists recognize that a major retreat of glaciers is happening worldwide. Of 612 glaciers in China alone, 53 percent are measured as retreating between 1950 and 1970.

World Climate Conference, 1979
In Geneva, the first of these conferences adopts climate change as a major issue. It calls on the world's governments to "foresee and prevent potential man-made changes in climate that might be adverse to the well-being of humanity."

1970, the first Earth Day
An environmental movement is established by Senator Gaylord Nelson of Wisconsin to spread concern about the planet. About 20 million Americans join in; by 1990, more than 200 million people in 141 countries are taking part.

Carbon emissions, 1989
Carbon emissions from fossil fuel burning and industry exceeds six billion tons per year. Globally today, more than 36 billion tons of CO_2 are emitted per year, with just 15 countries responsible for three-quarters of emissions.

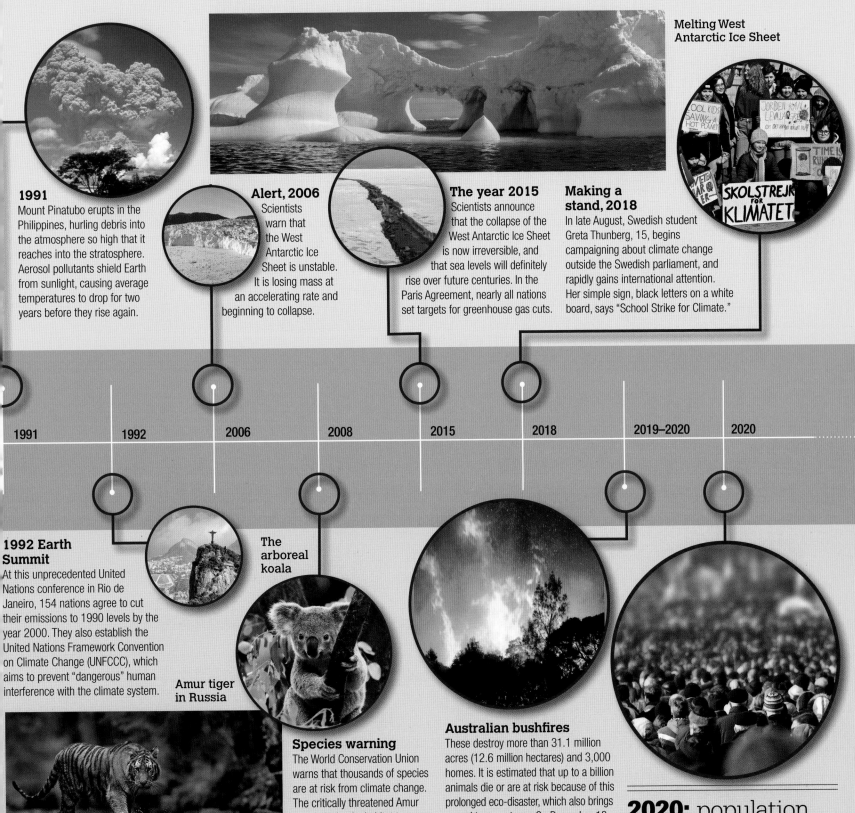

Melting West Antarctic Ice Sheet

1991
Mount Pinatubo erupts in the Philippines, hurling debris into the atmosphere so high that it reaches into the stratosphere. Aerosol pollutants shield Earth from sunlight, causing average temperatures to drop for two years before they rise again.

Alert, 2006
Scientists warn that the West Antarctic Ice Sheet is unstable. It is losing mass at an accelerating rate and beginning to collapse.

The year 2015
Scientists announce that the collapse of the West Antarctic Ice Sheet is now irreversible, and that sea levels will definitely rise over future centuries. In the Paris Agreement, nearly all nations set targets for greenhouse gas cuts.

Making a stand, 2018
In late August, Swedish student Greta Thunberg, 15, begins campaigning about climate change outside the Swedish parliament, and rapidly gains international attention. Her simple sign, black letters on a white board, says "School Strike for Climate."

1991 1992 2006 2008 2015 2018 2019–2020 2020

1992 Earth Summit
At this unprecedented United Nations conference in Rio de Janeiro, 154 nations agree to cut their emissions to 1990 levels by the year 2000. They also establish the United Nations Framework Convention on Climate Change (UNFCCC), which aims to prevent "dangerous" human interference with the climate system.

The arboreal koala

Amur tiger in Russia

Species warning
The World Conservation Union warns that thousands of species are at risk from climate change. The critically threatened Amur tiger is losing its habitat to deforestation, plus the increasing numbers of wildfires in a warming climate.

Australian bushfires
These destroy more than 31.1 million acres (12.6 million hectares) and 3,000 homes. It is estimated that up to a billion animals die or are at risk because of this prolonged eco-disaster, which also brings record temperatures. On December 18, 2019, it is the hottest day in Australian history, with an average temperature of 107.4°F (41.9°C).

2020: population reaches **7.8 billion**.

Volcanic weather

The astronauts of the International Space Station snapped this incredible picture of the Sarychev volcano, northeast of Japan, in early eruption in 2009. When a big, explosive volcano erupts, it blasts vast quantities of gas, dust, and ash into the air. Suddenly, the clear air is full of muck, and this muck is good at collecting water droplets. The volcano creates a vast thundercloud, and unleashes lashing rain, lightning flashes, and rolling thunder.

The biggest volcanic eruptions can cool the world. While ash from smaller eruptions is trapped in the lowest layer of the atmosphere and is soon washed out by rain, a big blast can punch the ash right through to the stratosphere. Then it can spread far around the globe, enveloping the Earth in a cloud that blocks out the Sun.

The eruption of Mount Pinatubo in 1991 caused a dip in global temperatures in the following year or two. The massive eruption of Mount Tambora in 1815 lowered global temperatures by as much as 5.5°F (3°C). In Europe, they called 1816 the "Year Without a Summer." Harvests were decimated and many people died of starvation.

Even milder eruptions may leak volcanic fumes full of sulfur dioxide. The sulfur dioxide then combines with moisture to create sulfuric acid, and the sulfuric acid creates a volcanic fog or "vog," damaging to human health.

Iceland's beautiful ice is retreating. **It may have largely vanished in a hundred years** from now.

OUR CLIMATE IS CHANGING

GLOBAL CHALLENGE

In the past, scientists talked only of global warming. Now they talk of climate change because all the extra heat energy is making climates behave wildly, with extreme temperature swings and stormy weather.

World temperatures rising:

Scientist have identified many signs that the climate is changing. The first one they noticed and the easiest to measure is global warming. Earth's average surface temperature has risen about 2.07°F (1.15°C) since the late 19th century, and five of the warmest years on record have occurred since 2010.

Melting home
Antarctica had record highs in 2020, soaring over 68°F (20°C).

SIGNS OF CLIMATE CHANGE

Warming oceans: The oceans have absorbed the extra heat, with the upper layer warming over 0.4°F (0.2°C) since 1969—and oceans warm very slowly.

Shrinking ice and glaciers: Greenland lost 286 billion tons of ice a year between 1993 and 2016, while Antarctica lost about 127 billion tons. Glaciers are retreating rapidly in most places.

Less snow: There's less snow than half a century ago, and it melts earlier each spring.

Vanishing sea ice: The Arctic ice has shrunk dramatically in the last 20 years.

Rising sea levels: The oceans have risen 8 ins (0.2 m) over the last century, and they've risen twice as fast over the last 20 years.

Extra humidity: The atmosphere has become more humid as global temperatures rise. This makes the air feel hotter, and more stormy.

Extreme weather: Record storms and record temperatures occur with increasing frequency.

Ocean acidification: The oceans are gaining 2 billion tons of carbon dioxide a year. All the extra carbon dioxide has made the oceans 30 percent more acidic than two centuries ago.

HARMFUL GASES

GREENHOUSE EFFECT

The world's climate is getting warmer and more energetic because of certain gases in the air. These "greenhouse" gases trap heat inside the atmosphere. They've always been there, keeping the Earth cozy. But now there's a lot more, thanks to human activity. Two gases especially are causing problems—carbon dioxide and methane. We put a lot of these two gases into the air when we burn fossil fuels—oil, coal, and natural gas.

Triple threat

Carbon dioxide rising: In early 2020, scientists found that 415 molecules out of every million molecules in the air is now carbon dioxide (CO_2). That doesn't sound like much, but it's a huge increase on the 280 molecules of 150 years ago. It comes mainly from burning oil, coal, and gas to generate electricity for industry and for powering cars, trucks, and planes. Methane rising: Methane is 30 times more powerful as a greenhouse gas than carbon dioxide. There's much less of it but it's gone up 150 percent in the last few centuries. Livestock farming is one reason—there's a lot of methane from cows—but a lot escapes, too, when oil and gas are taken from the ground, particularly during fracking. Water vapor rising: is the most abundant of all greenhouse gases. Most gets there naturally by evaporation from the sea. But as the world's climate warms, so the air takes up more water vapor, adding more warmth.

New clothes
are made in ways that generate CO_2 and waste water

Air travel
is one of the fastest growing sources of greenhouse gases

Livestock farming
Cattle and other livestock give off methane gas

If Earth's **entire atmosphere** was **carbon dioxide**, we would be just like **Venus**, the **hottest planet** in our **solar system**.

Hurricane Harvey dropped **historic amounts of rainfall** over southeast Texas in 2017, **way higher than would be expected** in a world that was not **warming**.

THE IMPACT

EXTREME WEATHER EVENTS

Climate change is already having a big impact. In early 2020, massive fires burned all over Australia, killing more than a billion animals. At the same time, Antarctica recorded its highest-ever temperature of over 68°F (20°C), causing a lot of the ice to melt. Meanwhile, other places suffered unusual storms and flooding.

Climate chaos

Climate scientists knew climate change would bring worse weather, but these events were even more extreme than expected. So, many scientists now talk about climate chaos. They can predict some things will happen; but the wilder climate means many events will still take us by surprise.

On December 18, 2019, Australia experienced its hottest day ever, reaching a high of 107.4°F (41.9°C).

In February 2020, Antarctica experienced temperatures of over 68°F (20°C), making a lot of ice melt.

LIKELY IMPACTS

Stormy times: Hurricanes and other storms will become more powerful and more common, bringing strong winds, very heavy rain, and flooding.

Droughts: Droughts and floods will both become more common.

Heat waves: Record-breaking summers will be the norm.

Wildfires: As summers get longer and drier, massive wildfires are more likely.

Melting ice: As polar ice melts, they will reflect away less of the Sun, speeding up warming. Water from the ice will raise sea levels.

Melting permafrost: Permanently frozen ground will melt, releasing methane gas, and accelerating global warming.

Rising seas: As heat swells oceans, and ice sheets melt, the seas will rise by 3.3 ft (1m), flooding low-lying coastal areas.

Mass extinctions of wildlife: Climate change will alter habitats, making some species extinct.

Mass migrations: Some places will become uninhabitable, forcing many people to move.

Food shortages: Many crops will not grow as well.

Water shortages: Water shortages will become more frequent and severe.

WILDFIRE

UNCONTROLLED COMBUSTION

Fires are a natural feature of dry forests and scrubland. Many wildfires start naturally in very dry conditions, often sparked by a lightning strike. As the world has warmed, with higher temperatures—including at night—and lower humidity, so has its potential to burn. The wildfire season is getting longer and the affected area is larger.

WILDFIRE JUST AHEAD

Fire warnings

A spark, dry fuel (such as twigs), plus oxygen can trigger an inferno, firefighters call this the "fire triangle." Within seconds, flames can be spreading at 14 mph (23 km/h), turning forests to ash and threatening whole towns.

American wildfire

Wildfires burn more than five million acres of land in the US each year. This one is in northern Nevada, but these fires also hit California, Montana, Idaho, Wyoming, Washington, Colorado, and Oregon with great frequency. Many are started by people, either carelessly or deliberately setting fire to areas that are bone-dry from a lack of rain. The cost in lives and money can be enormous.

Deadliest wildfires

Wildfires happen all over the world wherever hot, dry weather creates the right conditions for ferocious flames to take hold. Here are some of the worst recorded firestorms.

October 1825
Miramichi, New Brunswick, Canada
300 killed
3 million acres (1.2 million hectares) burned

October 1871
Peshtigo Fire Wisconsin, US
2,500 or more killed
1.2 million acres (4.9 million hectares) burned

September 1881
Thumb Fire, Michigan, USA
280 or more killed
1 million acres (400,000 hectares) burned

August 1910
Great Fire, Idaho and Montana, US
87 killed
3 million acres (1.2 million hectares) burned

May 1919
Great Fire, Alberta and Saskatchewan, Canada
11 killed
5 million acres (2 million hectares) burned

Firestorm

A firestorm is a blaze so fierce it creates its own winds. As hot air from the blaze shoots up, it draws in storm force winds from all around, fanning the flames. Wildfires can generate winds 10 times stronger than the winds surrounding them. The terrible Peshtigo fires in Wisconsin in 1871 produced especially damaging firestorms.

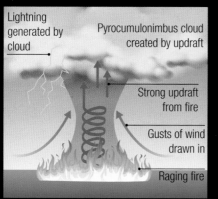

Lightning generated by cloud

Pyrocumulonimbus cloud created by updraft

Strong updraft from fire

Gusts of wind drawn in

Raging fire

Firenado

Scientists have long known about fire whirls (left), spiraling columns of flame that shoot up during a fire. But recently they discovered a much more frightening phenomenon—firenados. These are updrafts above a fire so huge and powerful that they actually make their own weather. The updraft creates a thundercloud, complete with thunder and lightning, and the cloud turns the updraft into a fiery tornado, dubbed a firenado.

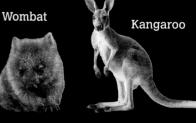

Wombat

Kangaroo

Fire beetle

Fire-adapted

Over the years, all kinds of creatures have adapted to live in the natural cycle of wildfires. Fire beetles fly toward fires and lay their eggs in dead trees. Wombats may allow other animals to shelter in their burrows, and kangaroos can move quickly to flee. Recent fires, though, have proved just too fast and too intense and many animals have perished.

Firefog

Wildfires can create superdense fogs. Smoke from a fire can send a lot of tiny ash particles into the air. These ash particles become condensation nuclei that make ordinary radiation fogs (*see pp. 74–75*) soup-thick. When drivers hit one of these on the road, it's as if they've suddenly gone blind. These fogs are to blame for many accidents in wildfire-prone areas.

January 1939
Black Friday bushfires, Victoria, Australia
71 killed
4.9 million acres (2 million hectares) burned

August 1949
Landes forest, southwest France
82 killed
124,000 acres (50,000 hectares) burned

1987
Black Dragon Fire, China and Russia
More than 200 killed
18 million acres (7.3 million hectares) burned

1997–1998
Indonesian forest fires, 70 million in 6 neighboring countries affected by haze
3.7 million acres (1.5 million hectares) burned

Summer 2014
Northwest Territories fires, Canada
0 killed
8.6 million acres (3.5 million hectares) burned

July 2018
Coastal areas of Attica, Greece
100 or more killed
3,100 acres (1,255 hectares) burned

Continent of fire

In December 2019 and January 2020, Australia was on fire (see p. 13). Record-breaking summer temperatures and months without rain fueled a series of huge wildfires across the continent. The scale and intensity of these fires was like nothing seen before.

At least 31.1 million acres (12.6 million hectares or 126,000 sq km) were burned. More than 33 people died and more than 3,000 people lost their homes. The effect on wildlife was truly tragic with over a billion animals thought to have been killed. Some species will probably be driven to extinction by the destruction of their habitat.

Across the world, from California to Russia, devastating wildfires seem to be breaking out more and more often—and they are getting bigger, too. Experts are certain the steady warming of the world's climate is to blame for these "megafires." The warmer climate makes for longer, drier summers, meaning there's more fuel for fires as plants grow and dry out, and also more lightning to spark them as thunderstorms become more frequent.

TOO DRY

HEATWAVES AND DROUGHTS

February is usually San Francisco's wettest month but in 2020, there was no rain in February at all! That might have been great for San Franciscans, but it's not-so-great for the planet's water cycle (see pp. 20–21). Less-than-average rain, and snow, reduces the groundwater, making soil drier, damaging crops, and causing water shortages.

Global water sources
This map shows what's been happening to global freshwater sources since 2002. The deepest reds show places where the average available freshwater has decreased the most.

DROUGHT

DRYING OUT

A drought is basically a lack of rain. Yet many weeks could go by in winter with no rain, and no-one would call it a drought. On the other hand, a month without rain in that crucial hot summer period when crops grow would be a disastrous drought for farmers, affecting how much food they can produce. But, the very same period could just be great vacation weather for others. Droughts are typically brought on by a long spell of hot weather or by too little snow in winter to melt in spring and fill the reservoirs. Droughts are the second-most costly weather events, after hurricanes.

High demand
Smart irrigation helps dry regions to get by with very little rain. It avoids wasting water by automatically monitoring weather, soil conditions, evaporation, and plant water usage to calculate new patterns of watering that change every day.

HEAT WAVE

DROUGHT MAKER

As our climate changes, extreme events are more common, especially droughts. But they affect places differently. In summer 2019 western Europe basked in a record-breaking heat wave, but the same weather brought disastrous droughts to East Africa and India. Later that year, Australia suffered its hottest, driest summer ever—followed by gigantic wildfires that burned for weeks.

"In 2012, **a heat wave and drought** in the Midwest had a more than **$30 billion impact.**"

Cooling off
In the center of Paris, people cooled off in fountains and even the Seine River in the record-breaking heat wave that reached 108.7°F (42.6°C). In the south of France, temperatures reached an all-time high of 114.8°F (46°C). The two heat waves claimed around 1,500 lives.

DUSTBOWL
SOIL DISASTER

In the 1930s, a combination of drought and intense farming practices turned much of the soil of southern Great Plains to dust. Huge, black blizzards of dust whipped across the surface and the area became known as the Dustbowl. Prolonged drought could see this phenomenon happen again.

Dust storm in Rolla, Kansas, May 6, 1935

Crop yields
If there is not enough moisture in the topsoil, plants will not even germinate. However, if the plants have enough moisture for early growth, as here, the final yield may not be affected if there is enough rainfall.

Weather influences
Impala gather to drink at a waterhole in the Mkuze Game Reserve in South Africa. The females have been known to delay giving birth if weather conditions are harsh. They also give birth in the middle of the day when the Sun is at its highest because that is when their main predators, lions, are resting.

Aeriel view of a waterhole

WATER SOURCES
DROUGHT SURVIVAL

Even drought-tolerant animals and plants struggle when there are record-high temperatures and a lack of rainfall. As droughts become more frequent, plants and wildlife have to develop strategies or migrate farther to find water. In Tanzania, scientists have observed elephants, plains zebras, warthogs, and yellow baboons digging waterholes that they use for only up to two weeks. This probably reduces the risk of infection from pools or rivers that have not been refreshed by rain.

BILLION-DOLLAR WEATHER

STORM STORIES

The worst weather can wreak havoc, destroying anything in its path. Between 1980 and 2019, 258 major weather and climate disasters hit the United States. More than 10,000 people died, with many more injured or displaced, and each disaster cost more than $1 billion. As the climate changes, many fear this pattern will get worse.

Type of disaster: Hailstorms
When: July 4–5
Where: Colorado
Damage: destruction of homes, vehicles
Cost: $1 billion

A disastrous year
2019 was one of the worst years on record, with 14 weather and climate disasters across the US. Flooding, severe storms, tropical cyclones, and wildfires resulted in the deaths of 44 people and will have significant long-term social and economic effects on the affected areas.

Type of disaster: Wildfires
When: Summer–fall
Where: California, Alaska
Damage: loss of power to millions of homes and businesses; loss of forests
Cost: $4.5 billion

Type of disaster: 190 tornadoes, Including an EF-4, hail, winds
When: May 26–29
Where: Rockies, central and northeastern states
Damage: houses and other structures destroyed across 12 states
Cost: $4.5 billion

Type of disaster: Hailstorms
When: March 22–24
Where: Texas, Oklahoma
Damage: destruction of homes, businesses, and vehicles
Cost: $1.6 billion

Type of disaster: Numerous tornadoes up to EF-3, high winds, hail
When: October 20
Where: Texas and central states

Damage: Destruction of houses, businesses, and vehicles across six states
Cost: $1.7 billion

Type of disaster: Tropical storm Imelda
When: September 17–21
Where: Texas
Damage: thousands of homes, businesses, and vehicles destroyed by flooding
Cost: $5 billion

Type of disaster: heavy precipitation

When: March 14–31

Where: north central states

Damage: flooding destruction of millions of acres of agriculture, as well as cities and towns; damage to roads, bridges, and dams across eight states

Cost: $10.8 billion

Type of disaster: Severe weather

When: May 16–18

Where: central states

Damage: Homes, businesses, and vehicles across four states

Cost: $1 billion

Type of disaster: Severe weather

When: February 23–25

Where: southeast and northeast states, Ohio Valley

Damage: major river flooding and high wind damage to buildings and farmland across 14 states

Cost: $1.3 billion

Type of disaster: Flooding due to record-breaking winter rainfall

When: March 15–July 31

Where: Mississippi River, affecting Iowa, Illinois, Missouri, Mississippi

Damage: crops, homes businesses, and river traffic suspended

Cost: $6.2 billion

Type of disaster: Hurricane Dorian

When: August 28–September 6

Where: Bahamas, Florida, Georgia, South and North Carolina

Damage: winds up to 185 mph (300 km/h), tornadoes and flooding destroyed homes and businesses

Cost: $1.6 billion

Type of disaster: More than 75 tornadoes, severe storms, hail, high winds

When: April 13–14

Where: southern and eastern states

Damage: destruction of homes, businesses, and vehicles across eight states

Cost: $1.3 billion

Type of disaster: Flooding due to heavy rainfall

When: May 20–June 14

Where: Arkansas, Oklahoma

Damage: Arkansas River and tributaries burst through levees, flooding many homes

Cost: $3 billion

Type of disaster: Severe weather, persistent storms, tornadoes, hail

When: May 7–13

Where: southern and southeastern states

Damage: houses, buildings and other structures across eight states

Cost: $1.5 billion

24 HOURS
of saving energy

Our carbon footprint is a way of measuring the amount of carbon we each release into the atmosphere because of our lives. You can significantly reduce yours by thinking a little differently about some of the things that you might do every day. Coal, oil, and natural gas are burned to make the energy we use, releasing CO_2 into the atmosphere. So the biggest win is just to use a little less energy! Here are some things you can do . . .

Are you in charge of the doing the dishes? Think about running your dishwasher only when it's full, rather than lots of times with small loads!

A shower uses way less energy than a bath. And usually takes less water. And you will get super clean either way.

Sleep well knowing that you did some great stuff for your planet today!

Air travel is carbon intensive, and some food is flown right around the world. You could think about making dinner with food that comes from somewhere more local instead.

New look? Making clothes takes a lot of energy, so take those you don't need to the thrift store so someone else can enjoy them. You could pick a new look there, too!

Have you thought about using energy-efficient light bulbs at home? Some use up to 80 percent less electricity and can last up to 25 times longer.

If you're the last person to leave a room, remember to switch off the lights!

If you have a school report to hand in and your teacher's fine with it, print double-sided to use less paper.

Does your school recycle? Lots of trash can be made into other things.

11:00 P.M.

9:00 P.M.

8:00 P.M.

7:00 P.M.

6:00 P.M.

5:00 P.M.

4:00 P.M.

3:00 P.M.

Open the drapes and let in the sunshine! Maybe you can save on using the warm air system to heat your home.

Close the refrigerator door while you get breakfast, and if you're drinking tea or coffee, try to only boil the amount of water you need for your drink.

Use less water. Don't leave the faucet running while you're brushing your teeth.

7:20 A.M.

7:30 A.M.

8:00 A.M.

8:30 A.M.

9:00 A.M.

10:00 A.M.

1:00 A.M.

Turn off the lights and fans before leaving the house. And make sure all your windows are closed. That way, your home will retain its heat and maybe you can use less from your system.

You can control how you heat your home remotely, so you can use energy only when you really need it. Some smart thermostats can even be programmed via smartphone apps.

72°F

You might already take the school bus, but if you travel in a car, consider walking or taking public transportation sometimes. Some people also choose to drive more slowly because it uses up less fuel.

Check air vents, if you can, with an adult, and safely. Blocked vents use up a lot of energy trying to pump hot air. You can also put on extra clothes instead of turning the heat up!

Don't leave your computer on standby when you grab lunch.

Unplug any chargers when your devices don't need charging. Chargers use power even when they're not in use.

STOP

WEATHER HEROES

FROM ACROSS THE WORLD

Cleveland Abbe (1838–1916), or "Old Probabilities" as he became known, gave the first official US weather report back in February 1871, after creating a public weather service in Cincinnati. Nowadays, the meteorologists who appear on TV when disaster strikes provide a vital service. And for centuries, women and men have gone to some extreme lengths to tell us about our weather. It's hard to choose, but here are some all-time weather heroes.

JUNE BACON–BERCEY

1928–2019

She was fascinated by science even as a young kid and became the first African–American woman to earn a degree in meteorology, at UCLA.

Big moment
In 1971 a Buffalo broadcast station was thrown into disarray when its anchor robbed a bank. Bacon–Bercey stepped in and correctly predicted a heat wave, by many accounts the first African–American woman to deliver the weather as a trained scientist. She was an immediate hit.

TETSUYA FUJITA

1920–1998

Tetsuya Fujita was a Japanese meteorologist who moved to the United States. Perhaps more than anyone else, he increased our knowledge of powerful storms, especially tornadoes.

JIM CANTORE

1964–

Obsessed by the weather since he was a kid, Jim Cantore (1964–) has worked at The Weather Channel for his whole career. As a forecaster, he researches data, and as a broadcaster, it's his job to let the public know about big storms and weather events in a way that's easily understood. With updates.

Storms
Fujita introduced the concept of tornado families and gave us the scale that links damage and wind speed. It's hard to imagine where the study of severe storms would be without him.

Hard work
Cantore has said that the hardest part of his job is getting up at 3:15 a.m. every day to read all the information about the weather that day.

Tornado in Colorado

Invented the Fujita scale for tornadoes

ADA MONZÓN

From Puerto Rico, Monzón is the Chief Meteorologist for WIPR TV. She is the first woman from Puerto Rico to be named a fellow of the American Meteorological Society.

Hurricane Irma
In 2017, Monzón followed Hurricane Irma as it passed near the Caribbean and then provided essential information and advice to the people of Puerto Rico during Hurricane Maria, a Category 5 Hurricane that devastated the island.

ALFRED WEGENER

1880–1930

Wegener (1880–1930) was a German scientist and record–holding balloonist! Because he liked balloons so much, he pioneered using them to track weather and air masses.

Expedition

Wegener went on several expeditions to Greenland to try and prove the existence of the polar jet stream. He died there while returning from an expedition to bring food to a group of researchers. He is also famous for his theory of continental drift: that Earth's continents are on the move.

DANIEL GABRIEL FAHRENHEIT

1686–1736

Fahrenheit (1686–1736) was brought up in Germany. When his parents died on the same day, in 1701, he was sent to Amsterdam to work for a merchant. He became fascinated by scientific instruments, traveling widely to observe scientists and makers.

Thermometer inventor

Fahrenheit became the first person to use mercury in a thermometer and invented the scale still used today, where the freezing point of water is 32°F and its boiling point is 212°F.

DR. JOANNE SIMPSON

1923–2010

As a child, Dr. Simpson loved sailing her catboat off Cape Cod and watching the clouds. She became a student pilot during World War II and had to learn about meteorology, which she ended up teaching to cadets. She went on to become the first woman in the US to hold a PhD in meteorology.

Cloud model

Among many achievements, Simpson explained how heat and moisture is distributed away from the Tropics and shed light on hurricanes. She developed the first computer cloud model, and at NASA was the chief scientist for the TRMM satellite, which studies tropical rainfall.

Weather research for the future

In late 2019, NASA launched the ICON spacecraft to the ionosphere, the region of the upper atmosphere where our weather meets space weather, to find out more about how the two interact.

This image, taken from the International Space Station (ISS), shows bright streaks of red "airglow" in the ionosphere, caused as the Sun's radiation charges (ionizes) the atoms and molecules of this layer as they travel through in giant winds. These winds can change on a wide variety of time scales—due to Earth's seasons, the day's heating and cooling, and incoming bursts of radiation from the Sun.

The turbulent and ever-changing ionosphere is home to the ISS and is the area through which radio communications and GPS signals travel. Variation there can result in distortions or even complete disruption of signals.

ICON is orbiting Earth every 97 minutes, between 55 miles (88.5 km) and 360 miles (580 km) above the surface. It's about the size of a refrigerator. Have a look out for what it discovers about the tug of war between our planet and the nearest region of space.

absolute zero
The lowest temperature that anything can reach.

aerosol
A solid or liquid particle suspended in a gas, such as mist in the atmosphere.

air mass
A large body of air covering much of a continent or ocean, in which the temperatures, pressure, and humidity are fairly constant.

air pressure
The pressing force of air created by its weight. Also known as atmospheric pressure.

albedo
The reflectivity of a surface; the proportion of incoming radiation that a surface reflects.

Earth's atmosphere

altitude
The height of something above sea level on Earth.

anemometer
An instrument used for measuring wind speed.

anticyclone
An area of high pressure, or "high," from which winds spiral out. It is created by cool, descending air and brings clear, fine weather.

atmosphere
The layers of gases surrounding Earth, stretching about 600 miles (1,000 km) into space and bound to Earth by gravity.

aurora
Bands of colored light in the night sky near the north and south poles. In the northern hemisphere they are called the aurora borealis or northern lights. In the southern hemisphere, they are called the aurora australis or southern lights.

barometer
An instrument for measuring air pressure.

Beaufort scale
A scale ranging from 0 (calm) to 12 (hurricane) that measures the force of the wind.

blizzard
A snow storm with winds of at least 35 mph (56 km/h) that lasts at least three hours.

carbon dioxide
A colorless, odorless gas found in the atmosphere that plays an important role in the greenhouse effect.

climate
The typical weather of a particular place or region, averaged over at least thirty years.

cold front
A boundary between cold and warm air masses, where the cold air is moving forward to undercut the warm air

condensation
The change from a gas, such as water vapor, to a liquid, such as water, caused by cooling.

convection
The circulation of air (or a fluid) caused by heat, in which warmer, lighter air rises and cooler, denser air sinks.

Barometer

cyclone
A rotating storm created by an area of low pressure, or "low," which draws winds in.

deforestation
The destruction of forests for their timber, or to clear land for farming.

density
How much of a substance is packed into a particular volume. The more there is packed in, the denser and heavier it is.

dew point
The temperature at which water vapor in the air will condense.

doldrums
A zone at sea around the equator where there is complete calm or only light winds.

dropsonde
A parachute carrying weather instruments dropped from a plane into storm to collect data.

drought
An unusually long period during which little or no rain falls, which causes serious shortages of water.

evaporation
The change from a liquid into a gas, for example water evaporates into the air when heated by the Sun.

extinction
The permanent disappearance of a species of animal or plant after the last of that species has died out.

eye
In a hurricane, the clear, calm zone at the center of the storm.

fog
A thick cloud of tiny water droplets close to the ground that reduces how far you can see.

fossil fuels
Carbon-based fuels, including coal, oil, and natural gas, that are made from the remains of organisms that lived millions of years ago.

front
The boundary between two air masses, where changes in weather usually occur.

frost
White ice crystals that form on cold surfaces when moisture in the air freezes.

glacier
A slowly moving mass or river of ice that forms as snow piles up in valleys over the years and compacts into solid ice.

global warming
The gradual warming of Earth's climate caused by build-up in the air of greenhouse gases which trap the Sun's heat, mainly from the burning of fossil fuels.

gravity
The force of attraction that pulls things together and makes things fall to the ground.

greenhouse effect
The way certain gases in the air stop the Sun's heat escaping back into space again, making the atmosphere warmer.

greenhouse gases
Gases in Earth's atmosphere that play a part in the greenhouse effect. The most important greenhouse gases are carbon dioxide and water vapor.

Clouds (mammatus)

GLOSSARY

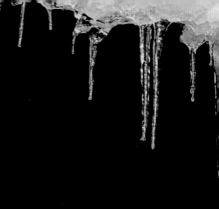

Icicles

gyre
An ocean current that goes round in a giant loop.

hail
Pellets of ice that fall from clouds.

heat island
An urban area with temperatures higher than the surrounding region because of factors such as the high absorbtion of solar energy by asphalt.

hemisphere
Half of Earth. Earth has northern and southern hemispheres.

hibernation
When animals spend the winter in a deep sleep or a sleep-like state called torpor.

high
See "anticyclone." Winds blow out clockwise in the northern hemisphere and counterclockwise in the southern hemisphere.

humidity
The amount or proportion of water vapor in the air.

hurricane
An intense tropical cyclone that occurs in the Caribbean and north Atlantic.

ice age
An especially cold period in Earth's history when ice sheets extended far out from the poles.

iceberg
A large chunk of ice broken off a glacier or ice sheet and floating on the sea.

ice sheet
A large mass of land ice that covers most of the underlying bedrock.

icicle
A tapering mass of ice formed by the freezing of dripping water.

IPCC
Intergovernmental Panel on Climate Change, established in 1988 to assess scientific information in order to understand and advise on climate change.

isobar
A line on a weather map that joins places with the same air pressure.

ITCZ
Intertropical Convergence Zone, the low pressure band in the tropics where trade winds converge from north and south.

jet stream
A band of very strong winds in the upper atmosphere.

landfall
The point at which a hurricane's eye crosses land after forming over water.

low
An area of low pressure or depression into which winds blow counterclockwise in the northern hemisphere and clockwise in the southern hemisphere. See also "cyclone."

meteorite
A meteoroid that reaches Earth's surface instead of burning up in the atmosphere.

meteorologist
A scientist who studies weather and climate.

meteorology
The scientific study of the weather.

methane
A colorless, odorless gas that is one of the greenhouse gases.

migration
The movement of people or animals from one place to another over long distances, often seasonal.

monsoon
The annual pattern of wet and dry seasons in India and southeast Asia and other places in the tropics.

NOAA
National Oceanic and Atmospheric Administration, an agency of the US Department of Commerce that conducts environmental research.

ocean current
A steady flow of seawater. Surface currents are driven by the wind. Deep currents are driven by differences in water density, related to temperature and salt content.

ozone layer
A thin layer of ozone gas in the upper atmosphere that filters out harmful ultraviolet rays from the Sun.

photosynthesis
The way in which plants make food by using the energy in sunlight to turn carbon dioxide and water into sugars, releasing oxygen in the process.

pollution
Anything that contaminates the natural world and harms living things. Pollutants include gases that escape into the air.

precipitation
Water or ice that falls or condenses on or near the ground, including rain, snow, hail, dew, and fog.

radiation
Emissions of energy in waves or rays or particles.

radiosonde
A balloon-borne instrument used to make and transmit measurements of temperature, humidity, and pressure.

Hurricane

GLOSSARY

Tornado

Saffir-Simpson scale
This describes how strong a hurricane is, based on how fast its winds are—the scale goes from Category 1 (least strong) to Category 5 (strongest).

smog
A thick fog caused when fog combines with air pollution

snowflake
A single flake or crystal of snow.

storm surge
An unusual rise in the sea caused by the low pressure of a storm, which may bring devastatingly high tides to coasts.

supercell
A giant moving thunderstorm that can create a tornado.

thermal
A rising column of warm air.

tornado
A violently spinning funnel of air descending from a supercell. The pressure in the center may be extremely low.

transpiration
The evaporation of water from plants, mainly through the leaves.

tropical cyclones
Powerful rotating tropical storms that form over the sea, for example hurricanes and typhoons.

typhoon
A tropical cyclone that occurs over the Indian Ocean or west Pacific Ocean.

warm front
A boundary between warm and cold air masses, where the warm air is moving forward to ride up over the cold air.

waterspout
A column of spiralling air that forms over warm and usually shallow water. May also be a tornado crossing water.

water vapor
Water in the form of gas. Earth's atmosphere contains water vapor.

WMO
World Meteorological Organization, a United nations agency concerned with the international collection and distribution of weather and climate data.

Snowflake

GLOSSARY

Drought

INDEX

Hailstone

INDEX

**Weather
monitoring
station**

The publisher would like to give particular thanks to the following people for their help: Neal Cobourne, Ben Ffrancon Davies, John Goldsmid, Sarah MacLeod, Ben Scheffer, Ali Scrivens, Tim Scrivens, Steve Setford, Marybeth Kavanagh, and Emily Teresa.

ACKNOWLEDGMENTS